BORN TO FLY

BORN TO FLY

Fighter pilot MP Anil Kumar teaches us there is no battle the mind cannot win

Nitin Sathe

Vitasta

Published by
Renu Kaul Verma
Vitasta Publishing Pvt Ltd
4348/4C, Ansari Road, Daryaganj
New Delhi - 110 002
info@vitastapublishing.com

ISBN 978-93-86473-49-3

First Edition 2019
Sixth Reprint 2025

MRP ₹450

Cover and layout by Vits Press
Printed by Vikas Computer and Printers

Salut

When you were strapped
in the cockpit
you were the best in flying
in the course.

When you were trapped
in your body
you were the one
who stayed the course.

Of service before self
of never giving up
of dynamic immobility
of moving mountains
of Government machinery
of getting others to count
off their blessings.

Yet calling for help
to swat a fly.

The chocks are off
my friend
taxiing out.....
I'll catch up,
We all will.

–ARS Mendonca

Felled by a freak accident that left him totally dependent on others while still in the prime of his career, Anil Kumar delved deep into the inner recesses of his depressed mind before returning triumphant, after having found the true meaning of Life. Without being able to lift even a finger, Anil shows how he transformed his own life, inspiring others to do the same. Nitin Sathe gives us a 'proof template' in his stirring account of a fighter pilot who harnessed the power of positive thinking in the face of extreme adversity

—Wing Commander Rakesh Sharma

Ashoka Chakra, Cosmonaut, Soyuz T 11

Preface

Reheat... (afterburners on)... Rolling... (for takeoff)...

MP Anil Kumar was up and away. The sky was actually his limit now. Free of life, free to fly high, the world at his feet. It was a new beginning; it was also the end of an era—MP had been tethered for too long.

MP, my friend and batchmate from the National Defence Academy, passed away on May 20, 2014 in the wee hours of the morning. He had spent 50 years and 15 days on this planet, almost half of them in a wheelchair. He had been paralysed neck down in an accident in 1988 after which his life revolved around hospitals, rehabilitation, and his wheelchair.

The accident altered the course of his life as a fighter pilot in the Indian Air Force (IAF) but could not claim him entirely. The end came 26 years later, due to a blood cancer detected a few months short of his 50th birthday. Twenty-six years earlier the doctors had all but given up on him and he had defied them all. Now, the doctors again said there was no hope, no point fighting. Only a miracle could save him this time. All we could do was wait and watch him wither away.

MP's dream of joining the Indian Air Force began as a boy in the small hamlet of Chirayinkeezhu in Kerala, when he opted to join the Sainik School, Kazhakootam. After clearing a rigorous selection process at the end of his schooling at 16, he headed to the National Defence Academy (NDA) at Khadakwasla in Pune. On passing out of the NDA with flying colours, MP went on to the Air Force Academy (AFA) to specialise in aviation and flying. Here too he excelled and was soon commissioned as a Pilot Officer in the Fighter Stream of the flying branch of the IAF. By 1985, he was part of the fighting forces, enjoying life as a young officer posted in an operational flying squadron at Pathankot.

Two years later, the accident abruptly ended his life as a fighter pilot. He had been one of the most promising pilots of his time, an officer of high calibre—a thorough gentleman. Everyone believed he was headed high up in the air force hierarchy.

The next few years were spent trying to adjust to a lesser vision of life after which he was formally boarded out of the air force to become an inmate of the Paraplegic Home in Kirkee, Pune. He spent the rest of his life there with people like himself, some paraplegics and some quadriplegics. The board outside his room now read 'Flying Officer Anil Kumar MP, Retired'. He was barely 24.

But MP never ever retired. He never got tired despite his disability. His mantra for survival kept him going. His life was about grit, determination and willpower of the highest order. Most of us would wilt, confronted with a disability of that magnitude. His zest for life should be the guiding light for many in his situation and in fact for us all, able and disabled. That is why his story needs to be told. I do believe that he was truly India's Stephen Hawking.

In this book, I have endeavoured to chronicle the life and times of MP Anil Kumar. Getting the story together wasn't easy. I was lucky to lay hands on various articles that MP wrote about his own life and other subjects that ranged from sports to politics to the armed forces. A large number of MP's friends from school, the NDA and IAF poured out their stories and feelings about him. I only had to weave it all together. The credits would run into many pages and I would be sure to miss out someone inadvertently; therefore my thanks and gratitude to all those who helped me write this biography. Without their involvement and help in reconstructing MP's life, this book would never have been written. A very special thank you is in order for MP's family. They gave me permission to write this book and provided insights into MP's early life.

I was never so close to MP as to be called his friend at NDA during our training years. We were further distanced when I went on to fly helicopters and he, the fighters. My relationship with him really began when MP was in hospital in Pune and thereafter at the paraplegic home where he lived the rest of his days. I spent many an hour with him during my holidays in Pune. Our bond grew strong and we kept in touch through various media over the years, closely connected to what was happening in each other's lives.

His stoicism is evident in one of his emails to a friend enquiring about his health. 'My health? The less said the better... In fact, solitude and I have become as inseparable as Siamese twins! As they say, what cannot be wished away needs to be endured, preferably with one's chin up.' This was the 'never say die' attitude that enabled him to lead a productive life.

He took the news of his cancer squarely on the chin. He was aware that he would have to spend more time in hospitals undergoing chemotherapy and got down to planning for it. He also knew that the end was fast approaching. There was still so much to do, he always told the people around him. Just a week or so before he flew away, he dictated his Will to his close friends in the ICU. This document is written in inimitable MP style with attention to every last detail. He still had his thinking cap on. The cancer couldn't stop him getting his point across.

In his last few days at the hospital he was still arguing with the doctors about letting him get back to his computer as his mailbox would be overflowing and he had a lot of writing to do. He suggested that he be sent back to stay in his room with his computer close by, coming to the hospital for chemotherapy sessions. Sitting next to his bed, running my hands through his hair, I watched him slip in and out of coma. He would open his eyes and recognise people around him and his humour, wit and conversation would resume. Amazing character.

His 50th birthday was celebrated in style in the special corner of the ICU reserved for him. He decided who was to be called and gave us explicit directions on how the day was to be celebrated. I think that was the last time he was fully coherent, alive and kicking. He knew it was his last birthday on this Earth. His condition started to deteriorate rapidly after the birthday bash, and the end came just two weeks later.

He is free today. Free of his shackles, free to soar. In a way, we were happy: He was born to be free. He had been put to the ultimate test, and here too he came out on top. Everyone who knew him will miss him and admire him forever.

Happy landings, MP!

Last landing

DARKNESS. THE room seems to be going round and round. Let it rotate. There is so much to do. And so little time. My mailbox is overflowing. So many friends want to know how I am and what I am up to. I have to reply to them. There is so little time.

It is dark and hot. Very very hot. Is the room on fire or am I? I tell the attendant, 'AC ko minimum karo (turn the air-conditioner to the lowest temperature)'. Still no relief! There has been no pain or physical discomfort for a long, long time. What is this then? My insides are on fire. Bring me water. The attendant has brought the transparent glass bottle and put the sipper tube to my mouth. I can't sip. Everything is burning, spinning out of control.

2

The last time I did such a spin was from 30,000 feet. I was falling like a leaf from the skies. 'Full opposite rudder, stick moving centrally forward'... the instructor's words boomed in my ears. And my fighter aircraft was in control again.

I am flying in my beautiful MiG-21. It handles like a baby. I love every moment with this baby. The sky is the limit. No barriers here. The only thing you could hit is a bird. They too love to soar. I am going to fly again. Someone come and turn me around, please! I can't lie in one position for too long...

Is that a fighter aircraft I hear overhead? It's a SU-30. Night flying tonight. Wonder where the flyboys will meet after the flying is done. Sit and gossip at the bar? Or bounce someone for a drink? I too have a night mission to complete. No, wait! Not today. The weather is not good. Let me get this tiresome paperwork completed instead and then head home... Hey, what's that? Thud... Darkness.

Where is Amma? Has she made the fried fish as I like it, with the extra masala? That cat needs to be put on a diet. Sheeja! Don't sit on Acchan's lap! Don't you know he is your father? Where is my book? I have miles to go before I sleep...! Wait!! Is that light I see beyond the darkness...?

Flashback

JUNE 27, 1988. Nice weather to fly. MP had been sent to Ojhar near Nashik in Maharashtra to ferry a MiG-21 fighter to Pathankot. Hindustan Aeronautics Limited, Ojhar, is where they carry out major overhauls on the MiG, giving it a new lease of life. It was a shining new machine just out of the paint shop, all ready to take to the skies. But it had to be tested for air worthiness before it was ferried to base.

More experienced test pilots had already carried out the initial phase of testing and declared the machine airworthy. Now it was Anil's turn to check it thoroughly for operational fitness and take charge of the aircraft along with the documentation. He had taken along a team of technicians who were helping him with the paperwork and administrative formalities.

4

There had been inordinate delays. What was to be a quick trip to collect the aircraft and ferry it in a week or so turned into more than three weeks. The aircraft had some niggling problems, and MP now had the opportunity to discuss them with the chief test pilot, the famous cosmonaut, Wing Commander Rakesh Sharma. MP managed to impress the test pilot with his knowledge of the aircraft and its systems, and the problems were sorted out and the aircraft cleared for the ferry. But the weather gods didn't seem too happy to see MP leave, and delayed him further.

Finally all was clear and MP was strapped into the cockpit, his maps carefully prepared for the long haul home. He was happy to be going back to his squadron; he had missed all the fun for the past few weeks and all the operational flying.

Ojhar had been a good break from the routine though, thought MP as he taxied out of the dispersal to the runway, returning the salute smartly to the technicians on the tarmac who saw him off. He had managed to see a couple of good movies, visited the shrine at Shirdi and met some of his friends posted there. Besides that, there was so much to see and learn about the aeroplane at this repair depot. All systems checked and rechecked, MP finally took off for Pathankot 1,365 km away, in what was to be one of the last sorties of his life.

The screech of tyres spewing smoke that follows the thud of the impact on concrete was music to his ears. Perfect touchdown at Pathankot after an incident-free ferry. Jettisoning his tail-chute at the end of the runway, MP taxied back slowly to the squadron dispersal, trying to see what had changed in the few weeks he'd been away. He was excited to be back with his friends and squadron mates. There were so many stories about Ojhar to tell them.

'Mission accomplished, new aeroplane inducted into squadron', mused MP as the engine went silent. Opening his canopy, he got down sprightly from the aircraft. He caressed the smooth cool skin of the MiG with his gloved hands as if it was a horse after a wild ride. She had behaved like a beauty, thought MP as he went around the machine to do his after-flight checks. Tucking his white helmet under his arm, oxygen mask thrown over his shoulder, MP walked back to the crew room to be greeted by his mates.

He spent the evening getting his room in order. He had been out for 26 days and there was dust everywhere. Then he went over to the squash court and played a few games before retiring for the night. It had been some time since he had played. Tomorrow would be a busy day. He was scheduled for two missions in the morning and one at night. As he shut his eyes, he mentally prepared himself for the sorties.

June 28, 1988, the day of the fateful accident. In an article in *The Indian Express*, October 11, 1994, MP writes, 'My 26 days' temporary duty to HAL Ojhar has resulted in a massive backlog on the secondary duty front and I am determined to finish it as soon as possible. In the morning, I flew a couple of sorties as wingman to Wing Commander RK Ghosh, my Commanding Officer, and Squadron Leader AK Jain. Like an indefatigable jet engine, I beaver away at logbook and blue book reports. It is plain drudgery! Drudgery is the other side of fighter flying'.

Besides the two sorties of the morning, the day had been rather busy. It had been hot and humid and all the officers had to go to the railway station to see off a colleague who was moving on posting. The squadron was relieved of afternoon work after that and they all met up for the briefing for night flying, in the evening. The weather forecast was not too good, with a strong possibility of thundershowers.

Briefings over, everyone retired to the crew room till such time as clearance came from the meteorological section that it was good to go. Friendly banter between cups of tea and fresh lime juice continued as they waited patiently to walk to their aircraft. The shrill noise of the telephone startled MP and he picked up the receiver.

It was the Met Officer. 'Weather warning for thundershowers extended upto 2200 hours', he informed. MP promptly conveyed the message to Squadron Leader PI Murlidharan, the Flight Commander, who was catching up on some paperwork in his office. A quick decision was made. There was no point waiting late into the night for the weather to clear. Night flying was called off.

The boys now had some time to themselves since there was a late briefing the next day. Flight Lieutenant Sanjiv Yadav, recently married and an energetic young man, invited all the bachelors for a drink followed by dinner. Happy about the outcome of the evening, the youngsters trooped out of the squadron to go to their rooms for a quick change before they headed to Yadav's residence.

'You guys carry on', MP said to them. 'I'll join you a little later. I have a lot of work to catch up on and I'll be there by the time dinner is served.' All alone in the crew room, it was deathly quiet as he got down to his paperwork. He was in charge of compilation of monthly reports and returns. These had been pending due to his long absence and this was the best time to finish it, he thought.

In the same article in *The Indian Express*, MP writes, 'Despite the workload, I find myself in a ponderous mood. I mull over the question: what are the three qualities most essential for becoming a good combat pilot? My mind is deluged with an assortment of answers: Unequalled skills, unerring judgement (common sense plus intelligence) and unwavering dedication—in that order and in abundance'.

He continues, 'It may be argued that these are the sine qua non of every profession. Absolutely true. But no other profession requires these qualities in such enormous quantities as fighter flying does. That is why fighter pilots are a special breed of professionals. That is why they have an aura of invincibility about them. That is why fighter flying is an exacting and unforgiving profession. *Certainly an unforgiving profession.* Dangers lurk everywhere. Everywhere. Even on the ground', he concludes.

The quiet of the night was broken by a peal of thunder. The Met forecast was accurate, thought MP as he heard the patter of rain on the asbestos ceiling. He pushed himself to finish a little more work. The rain turned into a pelting hailstorm with claps of thunder. The lights went off, the entire base was in darkness.

There was no point waiting anymore. It would be a while before the power was restored. Switching on his torch, which was part of the night flying kit, MP searched for his briefcase and the keys to his Hero Honda motorcycle. After ensuring that the office was locked, he walked to the parking lot.

'I kickstart my motorcycle and head towards the officers' mess. Soon I am out of the squadron area in pitch darkness. The ferocity of the storm had diminished somewhat but the terrifying eeriness continues unmitigated. I can discern an element of hostility in the thunderstorm...The thunder sounds similar to a series of bombs exploding at 30-second intervals', he writes.

'Carefully, I tread through the waterlogged main road. The technical area gate is open. A strong headwind is driving rain into my face, hazing my vision. I have to strain my eyes to follow the headlamp.'

As he approached the gate just outside the technical area he suddenly saw a horizontal bar across the road. 'This wasn't there when I left for Ojhar' was the thought that flashed through his mind. Too late; he was less than 10 metres away. The only option and the survival instinct was to duck and try to sail under the bar and at least save his head. He did just that.

The guard manning the barrier was watching the scene unfold. He realised a little late that the rider had not seen the barrier in his path. He rushed to open the barrier. He struggled to push the bar down to disengage it from the inverted 'U' hook that bound it. Just as the barrier actually went down, MP was ducking his head to get under it. Bad timing.

Thud... Darkness.

THE MOTORCYCLE careened to the left as MP was thrown off, the bar of the barrier hitting the base of his helmet, pushing his neck back. The helmet was crushed, damaging his cervical bone and fracturing three of his vertebrae. He lay on the road whilst the guard looked around frantically for assistance. Since there appeared to be no bleeding, the guard thought there was no major injury.

A little while later a car came towards the mechanical transport section where it was to be parked for the night. The guard flagged it down and asked the driver to help get MP to station sick quarters (SSQ). The car was quickly turned around and the driver got down to help the guard lift the supine MP into the vehicle.

This is where the second 'accident' or mishandling occurred. 'When the duo lifted me, they just held me by my hands and legs, leaving my head hanging without support. Due to this, the base of the helmet pushed the fractured pieces of the vertebrae down into the spinal cord, thereby damaging it internally', writes MP.

He was taken to the SSQ, a few hundred metres from the accident site. MP regained consciousness, yelling in pain due to the severe distress caused to the neck. The doctors were immediately summoned and the helmet was removed with much difficulty. Care had to be taken not to aggravate the neck injury further. MP remembers, 'Despite the terrible pain, I tried getting up; and that is when I realised that I had been paralysed. I was shocked to death. It struck me *right away* that the paralysis could be due to the head injury'.

The doctors couldn't do much at the very rudimentary SSQ. With a few painkillers jabbed into him, it was decided to move MP to the military hospital located close to the perimeter of the airfield. Here too, there was no expert help available for such a complex spinal injury patient. A quick decision was made to transfer him to the army hospital in Delhi. The air force was quick to respond by arranging an airlift early the next morning.

His Flight Commander, Murli, writes, 'I rushed across to the accident site and then to MH Pathankot'. Speaking to the guard at the gate he realised there had been a slip-up in keeping one of the barriers down with the adjoining gate open. He continues, 'During the night we learnt that Anil's C4/C5 vertebrae had fractured; he was having difficulty breathing as his diaphragm wasn't functioning. I requested my brother Suvarthan, an IAS officer posted at Delhi, to take over and give us feedback on Anil's condition. His temperature kept shooting up and things didn't seem too good'.

Since the aircraft was to arrive early the next morning, one of the bachelors of the squadron was sent to MP's room to pack some clothes and toiletries in a bag that was to accompany him. In those times, the 'scoop stretcher' along with the traction equipment required for carriage of spinal injury patients was not available at the MH. The patient was simply fastened on to a hard board with straps, small sandbags around the neck for support. It worked well, but MP's case was severe and it was decided that it would be safer to get a scoop stretcher.

All efforts to procure one locally proved futile. A scoop stretcher was available at command hospital (CH), Udhampur, 70 km away. Flight Lieutenants Ranbir (Bira) and KR Ajit (Jita) agreed to go down to the hospital at Udhampur and get the stretcher on their motorcycle. They drove through the night and drove back by early morning, the contraption precariously balanced on one side of their bike. This was used to carry MP to the army hospital in Delhi.

At the Research and Referral Army Hospital located at Dhaula Kuan, the paramedics and spinal injury specialists were standing by, ready to attend to the special case arriving at noon. MP was immediately stabilised and taken for a very difficult surgery by veteran specialists, the best available at the time.

June 27, Chirayinkeezhu. MP's mother, Amma, felt suddenly uneasy and had a bout of vomiting. Sheeja, his sister, writes, 'The birds too chirped discordantly and the gloomy atmosphere made all of us feel ill'.

On 29th morning, news of the accident reached MP's father, Acchan. Visibly disturbed, he said not a word to anyone at home. He told Sheeba, the elder daughter, not to go for her classes and paced outside the gate. After a while, the younger Sheeja noticed a small crowd outside the house. A maternal uncle, Devadas, from the neighbouring village and a few other friends of her father had joined him. She thought it was one of their usual political discussions.

By noon, Amma and the children began to get worried. Something was not quite right. There was too much tension in the air. Acchan broke away from the group and slowly walked into the house. Standing at the door, he announced, 'Kunjumon has had an accident'. Amma wailed and fainted. A light had gone out of her life.

THE SURGERY continued for six long hours. The back of Anil's neck was opened up along the spinal column. The doctors had to be careful not to cause further injury to the nervous tissue. Small pieces of bone wedged in the tissue were removed one by one. The neck was sewed up and Anil was moved to the ICU for recuperative care.

As he awoke to severe pain above his neck, MP looked around for people he could speak to. Friends, doctors and nurses looked at him in a way that told him instantly that it was hopeless.

In one of his many returns to consciousness, he saw one of his classmates and another friend sitting next to him. Gathering all the energy he could muster, MP whispered that he had decided not to live anymore; would they help him? 'Please get me some poison that will kill instantly', he pleaded. They couldn't look him in the eye; they didn't know what to say. His schoolmate and course-mate from NDA, who sat closest to him, gathered his wits and said, 'Have courage. We will wait for five years and see how you progress. If you still want to die then, we shall see what can be done'. MP slipped into coma again.

Five years to the day, MP sent a mail to this friend. The pact made five years ago could be cancelled.

He had found reasons to live by then.

There was nothing much that could be done in Delhi after the surgery. The doctors could only wait and watch his recovery. It was decided to shift MP to the military hospital in Kirkee for further management.

Writing in *The Indian Express* in October 1994, MP says, 'When I regained consciousness, I found myself in the yoked world of quadriplegics. Now, I'm like a man fettered for life, unable to use my hands and legs, completely paralysed below the neck, incontinent, spoon-fed and totally dependent. Ironically, the most painful aspect of quadriplegia is the *painlessness. Willy-nilly* I'm now part of the micro-world inside the macro-world that is strictly governed by Charles Darwin's tenet of *Survival of the Fittest.* I am a live vegetable since that cruel night'.

2014. TWENTY-SIX years after the accident. MP was terminally ill. Acute myeloid leukaemia, the most dangerous form of blood cancer, had been confirmed. Despite doctors' advice against strong doses of chemo, MP chose to try it out as a last ditch effort to beat the disease. As a godsend, BS Krishna Kumar or KK was posted to NDA as head of training around the same time. He was MP's schoolmate, classmate and NDA course-mate. He was also in the same squadron as MP at NDA. Despite his demanding job, KK ran between hospital and academy over months, spending as much time as he could with MP, helping with his treatment and administrative requirements during his illness.

After his workday, KK would pack some food for MP and head to the hospital located 17 km away. MP would be slipping in and out of sleep due to the heavy medications. When he was awake and found KK beside him, MP would start discussing various aspects of his life. From his love for the actor Prem Nazir, to the pranks they played at school and NDA, his life in the village and various experiences with friends... It was as if he was rewinding his life, reliving all the good moments. As he tired himself out talking about the past, MP would slip into sleep only to wake up after a few minutes and continue his banter as if nothing had happened. It was during one such session with KK that MP expressed his desire to draft a Will.

The Will was to be dictated by MP but it needed some legal expression as well. Thomas Kutty Joseph, his school- and course-mate from NDA, was summoned. Joseph had recently retired from the army and begun practicing as a lawyer at the Supreme Court in Delhi. He drafted the basic outline of the Will and read it out to MP. MP dictated a few lines for insertion in the text at various places. KK was asked to get the draft typed and brought back for scrutiny the next day. KK remembers that MP was still not happy with the draft and wanted further changes. These were again incorporated and this exercise of iterations continued over the next few days.

Despite the chemotherapy that was taking its toll on his

body, MP's mind remained as sharp as ever. He remembered exactly what changes were required in the language and ensured that every comma and full-stop was just where he wanted it.

Phew! He was such a stickler for perfection even in his last days! The draft was immediately typed on stamp paper and signed by three witnesses—MP's brother, MP Jayakumar, Air Commodore Krishna Kumar, and Colonel RK Mukherjee. MP's thumb impression was affixed to the document. A photograph was also taken with all of them around his bedside after the deed was done.

The Will is thoughtfully crafted and beautifully written. It summarises MP's life in his inimitable style. It also reveals his personality, his upbringing, his compassion and love for life. When I read it for the first time just a few days after MP's departure, I shed a quiet tear or two.

Despite his disabilities, MP writes in his Will, he has discharged his responsibilities as a son and brother, and has been able to provide for the financial needs of the family, during his lifetime and after.

'As a quadriplegic with no control over my body below my neck for over a quarter century', he writes, 'I have understood the meaning of dependence, perhaps a shade more than ordinary persons, and basic life, as we quadriplegics live it, is based on the utter dedication and 24x7 continuous assistance rendered by attendants.' In gratitude and affection for his attendants, he leaves each a sum of money, bequeathing the rest of his financial assets to his mother, siblings and friends.

In a poignant reminder of how confined his physical world was, he distributes each of his few tangible assets. To the paraplegic institute that was his home for over two decades he left the ambulance bearing the 'Kazaks 81' logo of his school batch, all of whom contributed towards the vehicle to improve his mobility. He also left the home his air-conditioner and TV.

'It is my desire that my PC is not used by anyone and that the same is preserved along with a few mementos, photographs and two medals, namely the Best Air Force Cadet at NDA and Best in Aerobatics at AFA, that I cherish, preferably in a humble and non-ostentatious manner at my alma mater, SSKZM, so that the essence of my life, "disability need not defeat you", can be better understood by young minds.'

'Before concluding, I would like to add that despite limitations imposed by physical handicaps, life has been intellectually stimulating and satisfying on account of the effort and pains taken by so many of my classmates, batchmates, family, friends, all of whom can neither be mentioned nor adequately thanked, so simply signing off with a big Thank You.'

MP SEEMS to live on in the little corner of the Sainik School Kazhakootam where his belongings have been preserved just as he wanted them to be. A large poster hangs behind his wheelchair in the far-left corner of the enclosure, with one of his quotes under it: *Greater the difficulty... Sweeter the victory*. His medals and plaques are framed and mounted on the walls. So is his famous essay titled, 'Airborne to Chairborne'. Some of his other published articles and a few of his books are also displayed. To the right stands the special contraption that holds the computer, keyboard and mouth-writing implements that were MP's best friends for most of his later life. Next to the computer is his trunk from his NDA days, with his name painted on it.

The small enclosure is aptly named 'Turning Point'. Most of the children at the school have spent time here, reading about MP's life. When I visited the school in 2015, I projected a photograph of MP before I began my formal lecture to the students, and asked the boys if they knew the man. All hands went up in unison.

The memorial space has been designed and sponsored by MP's closest friends, G Prakash and Haridas. It was formally inaugurated by Lieutenant General Sarath Chand, Chief of Staff, Southern Command, on December 12, 2015, at a function organised by the Old Boys Association. Almost every member of MP's family was present at the inauguration, along with a large number of his classmates. The 'Late Flying Officer MP Anil Kumar Memorial Achiever Award' was instituted by the old boys on this occasion, the first being awarded to the eminent journalist Josy Joseph.

As I walked around the school campus, I came upon the derelict yellow Harward aeroplane which was donated to the school long years ago, where MP spent much of his time, sitting in the cockpit, wielding the jammed controls, dreaming of flying.

SOME 15 KM away from the school is MP's village, tucked away in an obscure corner, with the backwaters all around.

MP's home is a veritable memorial to him. As you enter, a large air force flag mounted on the wall greets you. Below that are clustered photographs of every stage in MP's life: as a baby, when he left for school, group photographs from his schooldays, NCC, NDA, his squadron at Tezpur and Pathankot. And then photographs of him in his wheelchair, the most recent being a portrait by a professional during the making of the documentary on MP's life produced by his classmates titled, *The Fight Goes On*.

In the bedroom he shared with his sister his mattress and pillows are preserved. His mother served me lunch in the plate that Anil used, though he had not been home for 25 years before he died. Every letter MP wrote home is preserved in a folder—the mouth-written ones from the first few years after the accident, and later the letters typed out on his computer. His published articles are preserved too, along with some diaries and notebooks. An invitation to the passing out parade at the Air Force Academy on December 21, 1984 slips out of one of them.

Rookies, at home and school

CIRCA 1964. Chirayinkeezhu, Kerala, a nondescript tehsil dotted with 29 villages, 35 km north of the district headquarters at Thiruvananthapuram. On May 5, to N Panchapakesan and SM Kamalamma, was born their first child. The family celebrated, and named the boy Madanavila Panchapakesan Anil Kumar alias MP. The soothsayer said the boy would achieve greatness. The family members looked at the baby and thought so too.

The village that MP and his siblings grew up in is a picturesque hamlet surrounded by the network of backwaters and canals so characteristic of the State of Kerala. It is largely a fishing village, with some coir and weaving industries. Over the years, mechanised weaving has all but destroyed the handloom industry. The area boasts greats such as Raja Ravi Varma, the prolific painter and social reformer, and Prem Nazir, actor and superstar.

The landscape is dotted with temples, most prominent being the Sarkara Devi Temple, famous for the Kaliyoot festival that originated in Travancore in 1748. A large number of Indian and foreign tourists visit the area for its peaceful and quiet beaches.

The only Indian State to maintain 100 per cent literacy, Kerala has a politically aware population, and has been a bastion of the Left. Politics and identity are intertwined and it is common to see particular communities leaning towards a particular political ideology. For example, the Catholics are generally supporters of the Congress and the Ezhava community leans to the Left. Chirayinkeezhu is one of the Left-supporting regions and Anil's family have also been supporters of the Communist Party. Two of Anil's friends in the neighbourhood are named Mao and Karl Marx!

As time went by, MP's parents were blessed with three more children: a son named MP Jayakumar followed MP after two years while the girls—MP Sheeba and MP Sheeja—were much younger. MP Jayakumar had a twin brother, who sadly did not survive.

While the children grew up, MP's father dabbled in local politics and became the village sarpanch in 1972. He kept in close touch with the big names in Kerala politics at the time but refused to enter State politics despite being urged to do so. His political mates included AK Gopalan, known as AKG, who was leader of the opposition in the Indian parliament for a while. He and many other political bigwigs were often at MP's home for discussions. Panchapakesan came from an erudite family of Sanskrit pundits. Three of his uncles were graduates almost a century ago, no mean achievement in their time. They were responsible for ensuring that every family in the village had at least one graduate. MP's mother remembers that these uncles served in the highest positions in the government, one rising to become secretary of the Public Service Commission of Kerala and helping a large number of village folk get permanent jobs, a legacy still recalled by many in the hamlet.

Panchapakesan remained devoted to this little settlement and did a lot for its development. He ensured that the panchayat was upgraded to a special panchayat with additional funds. He got buildings constructed in the marketplace, and a special road sanctioned to connect the village to nearby Trivandrum. This road entailed building a number of bridges over the waterways, greatly reducing travel time. In 1973, he pushed the government to upgrade the police outpost at the village to a regular police station. Another of his successful projects was cheap housing through the 'Lakh Housing Scheme' for the poor and needy. This popular State government housing scheme aimed to build 100,000 dwellings for the homeless.

In 1978, Kerala saw one of the worst floods in its history. Several parts of the village were inundated due to poor drainage. Panchapakesan saw to it that new gutters and channels were created all over the village to prevent such damage in future. He went from house to house to convince residents to give up an area of three feet in front of their homes for the construction of the water channels.

Around the same time, the collector and the local panchayat were having trouble controlling communal tensions between Muslims and Hindus who were squabbling over a piece of land for construction of a mosque. Panchapakesan stepped in and convinced both groups to solve the matter amicably, ensuring that the mosque was built without any further problems.

The Chirayinkeezhu panchayat was one of the first to have street lighting, and was considered a model panchayat by surrounding villages.

The Panchapakesan family lived in a small house in the centre of the village in the area called Valiyakada. The taluka hospital, railway station, bus stand, local market, banks and government offices were close by. The house had two sections. The one closer to the main road was the living area in the olden times, and now lies in ruins. A small pathway leads to another small dwelling where MP's mother now resides. A well stands in the middle of the property. In earlier times, this inner part of the house served as a guesthouse for the many visitors. The area around the house is lined with coconut, acacia, cashew, jackfruit, mango and tapioca trees.

A darkish, bubbly and chubby child, MP grew up quickly, eating his rice, avial, sambaar and fish. The watchful care of his mother and aunts ensured that a strong foundation was built to take on the rigours of later life.

The boy's first words were written on a slate with chalk dipped in water. His uncle painstakingly taught him to write and the young boy quickly acquired a distinctive cursive style. He loved to read any magazine, comic or book he came across. 'I used to see him reading from the little pieces of newspaper and magazines used to wrap and pack groceries', his Amma remembers. This was the beginning of his insatiable desire for knowledge. As soon as he was old enough to run, the boy was in the streets playing with friends.

Amma remembers the day MP went to school completely forgetting there was an exam. He was unprepared; his slate was broken. On seeing this, the master wrote a big zero on the slate and threw him out of the class. The boy was crestfallen and worried about how he would confront the family at home. He hung around so he could reach home at the usual time.

Meanwhile, a sneaky girl from his class ran home to Amma and told her what had happened. When MP got home he realised they knew what had happened and burst into tears. Acchan did not relent. MP got one whack on his backside and went without a meal that night!

It was very difficult to get stories about Anil's childhood from Amma. As soon as she began narrating something, tears would well up and we would have to change the topic. But she did tell me about the time they were walking back from a nearby village through a cashew plantation. The trees were full of ripe cashew apples and the smell beckoned MP to the fruit he loved. He insisted that a fruit be plucked for him and no amount of cajoling would take his mind off it. Anil went and sat on the nearby railway tracks and refused to budge till his demand was met. Finally, the uncle accompanying them was forced to climb a tree and steal a fruit for MP! 'This was the only time I saw my child so adamant and badly-behaved', Amma said.

N Sarojanan, MP's uncle and a confirmed bachelor, took MP under his wing and was extremely fond of the young boy. It was he, in a manner of speaking, who decided the boy's destiny. He suggested that MP be sent to a good school to receive a better education and persuaded MP's father to consider Sainik School. The first four years of MP's school life were spent at the 110-year-old Malayalam village school near his home, the Palavila Government Lower Primary School. It had about 100 students and a handful of teachers then. Sarojanan died of leukaemia when MP was 12 years old. Till such time he was fit, however, Sarojanan took it upon himself to pick up and drop MP to and from school in a taxi. He also frequently took him for outings, remembers Sheeja, adding, 'I wasn't happy about this at all since I was left out of these trips!' Sheeja remembers that one of MP's oldest friends was a skinny boy named Sisu. He belonged to a very poor family that sold vegetables in the local market. He lived right behind MP's house and not a day passed when the two were not together. Other friends—Baiju, Syamkumar and Sajeev—were much younger and addressed MP as Kunjannan, a variation of his petname at home, Kunjumon, meaning 'little one'. Some of the younger boys in the family also addressed MP as Anilannan. Many of his childhood friends dropped out of school and went abroad in search of livelihoods. Most got into business and are well-settled now. But MP proved to be a quiet and hardworking student. His teachers praised him, and MP's father was convinced that his uncle was right. Preparations began to get MP ready for the Sainik School written exam.

A schoolmaster, Madhavan Pillai Sir, was summoned to provide extra coaching. After just two or three classes, Madhavan Sir went up to MP's dad and opined that there was no need for further coaching. MP would rank within the first 20 in the merit list. The entrance exam wasn't easy. It included tests of intelligence, science, math and language ability. Once passed, an interview and medical exam followed. The students had to be physically and mentally robust to take on the rigours of pre-military training.

After his Class 4 exams, MP went through the admission process with ease and waited for the final merit list to be announced. It was the summer of 1973. He was the first boy from the family to attempt to join Sainik School, an institution that people in his village had only heard about. Madhavan Sir was wrong. MP's name was not in the top 20, more like the bottom 20. But get in he did. A total of 101 boys were selected to be part of what would be called the 'Kazak 81' group, the batch name that would stick to them all their lives.

Realisation dawned that he would have to leave home soon. MP was barely nine years old and couldn't really fathom the idea. All the elders and relatives would proudly remark, 'You will soon be leaving us and the village and going to an "English" boarding school'. Acchan would announce this proudly to everyone as he walked his son through the village.

His mind in turmoil, MP went up to his mother one day and asked, 'Will I be getting *pazhanjore* to eat at school?' His mother looked at him with moist eyes and smiled. Pazhanjore is a preparation made from rice fermented overnight and mixed with curries. He was already missing home!

The entire family joined in the preparations. A new trunk, some essential clothing and toiletries listed by the school were bought and packed. Amma also packed some sweets that could be eaten by the lad when he was alone, little knowing that the sweets would all be over in the first two days, shared with new found friends!

Sainik School

THE SAINIK School Kazhakootam is located about 18 km from Trivandrum, now Thiruvananthapuram, on NH47, leading north along the western coastline. The 225-acre campus stands on a hillock sandwiched between the Western Ghats and the Arabian Sea.

The undulating terrain, green surroundings peppered with coconut, acacia and cashew trees, and the fresh air provide just the right environment for young boys to grow into bright men in the eight years they spend here.

Founded in 1962 as the dream project of then Defence Minister VK Krishna Menon, this was one of the first five Sainik Schools to be set up all over India. Over time, the number has grown to 26 and there are plans to increase the number further to 43 in the near future, with at least two Sainik Schools in each of the major States. Menon's vision was to provide quality all-round education to intelligent students from rural areas and nurture them for induction into the armed forces of the country. The schools were therefore required to have the best infrastructure for training.

When I visited the institution in mid-2015, I realised that the campus does indeed provide an ideal environment for the military training of a young mind.

The motto of the school is apt: *Gyan*, *Anushashan*, *Sahayog*, meaning Knowledge, Discipline and Cooperation. NCC training is compulsory for all students and that helps them get oriented and motivated to don the uniform. Amongst the alumni in the school's hall of fame are Colonel NJ Nair (Roll No 71), Ashoka Chakra, Captain R Harshan (Roll No 2776), Ashoka Chakra, Second Lieutenant RM Naresh (Roll No 112), who lost his life in the famous tank battle on Munnawar Tawi in 1971, and Major GS Sateesh Chandran (Roll No 447), who laid down his life fighting militancy in Nagaland in 1992. All of them are posthumous awardees. The school also boasts a number of one-, two- and three-star generals who have done the armed forces proud and their names are prominently displayed on honour boards.

MP arrived at Sainik School Kazhakootam or SSKZM on a cloudy and humid morning in April 1973. With butterflies in his stomach, he travelled the short distance from his village in a taxi with his father and uncle. The sights, sounds and smells flashed past as he gazed out, not uttering a word throughout the journey.

He was worried about the English-medium school, so different from the village school where subjects were taught in Malayalam. How would he mix with boys from different parts of the country who didn't speak his language?

They stood in awe before the majestic academic block. The housemaster and matron welcomed the children. Anil waited with a group of unknown children around him, and Acchan got busy with the admission formalities. The children were made to stand in a line and were issued their kit. Anil had to check each item in the pile before him against the list provided. He looked around lost and saw that all the boys around him seemed to be in the same predicament. One concerned parent came forward to help his confused child. He was shooed away politely. 'The boys have to learn to look after their kit and equipment themselves', he was told by the matron. This was probably the first lesson in 'militariness' for the boys.

Their belongings were put away in a trunk that would fit exactly under the bed in the dormitory. This was to be their only big piece of luggage for the rest of their stay. The trunks were carried to the dormitories by the boys. The parents said tearful goodbyes and the boys were on their own. Their journey into life had begun. Kunjumon was now Cadet MP Anil Kumar-1122.

Roll numbers for this batch were allotted from 1055 to 1155; the odd ones went to Tagore House, the even numbers to Veluthampi House. Anil was allotted Roll Number 1122, and therefore he trudged to Veluthampi House with his luggage. This was to be his home for the first two years of school. It was a good idea to segregate the small boys for the initial period so that they could be 'broken in', learning to live with boys of different age-groups later.

The school routine began, keeping them so busy that they did not miss home too much. However, the first few days were spent weeping silently into their pillows, learning to wash their own underwear, sleep alone in their own bed, and sit at a table and eat in a group where no one knew anyone.

The roll numbers were to be stamped on each piece of clothing and kit by the student himself. He was provided a reed pen dipped in indelible ink. MP's number 1122 was stamped on all the items of the kit. It was stamped indelibly on his psyche too, staying with him throughout his life. To this day, the old boys recognise each other by their numbers, using their roll numbers in their email addresses and passwords too!

The roll number was used for almost everything at school—from the infirmary to the dhobi and cobbler. MP recalled how some of the naughtier boys used fictitious or nonexistent roll numbers when they were up to some mischief. 'The cobbler and canteen fellow used to bear the brunt of the tricks', remembered MP. 'One would go to the cobbler and get some repairs done or have a snack at the canteen and provide the number of someone who had passed out of the school ages ago or hadn't even been born!' The poor men were denied their earnings, but the school did compensate them eventually.

MP's housemaster was CK George, commonly called 'Country' or 'CKG'. He was a tough taskmaster, liberal in the use of the cane, and all the children were terrified of being confronted by him. They still wince when they remember the caning, but they all agree that 'the cane was painful, but it did put us on the right path more often than not'.

A typical day began with the housemaster walking down from his residence screaming, waking the boys up at 5 am sharp. The queues would soon form for the washbasins and the toilets after the sweet lukewarm tea with biscuits was gobbled down.

There was no time to lose; they had to be at the parade ground for muster prior to PT at 6 sharp. The first few mornings were full of panic, but soon the boys got used to the routine.

This is where the phrase 'After You Sir' originates, explains an ex-student. One could reserve one's position in the bathroom lines by tapping the person in front and saying the three magic words. So you could tap someone who was waiting in the line for the loo and go and brush your teeth at the washbasin until your turn came! If you weren't there when it was your turn, you moved back to the end of the line. 'This was another lesson in smart time management', explains the old boy.

After PT, it was time to get into uniform—cotton khaki shorts and shirts, starched and with shoulder flaps, metal badges and little berets with colourful plumes, all designed to add to the 'military' feel. There was a rush now for the mess. It was breakfast time. The mess was big enough to seat all of them together and each student had a fixed place in the dining room. Breakfast was to be eaten with clockwork precision. The boys wolfed down as much as they could in the time available and headed for seven long study periods.

On Monday morning there was drill instead of PT and also what was called the assembly parade. At this special assembly, patriotic songs were sung, followed by the principal's address. 'The ignominy of the parade was the caning of the "delinquents" by the masters in front of the whole school', explains an old schoolboy.

Lunch followed the classes at about 1.30 pm. And then the kids got their first break of the day. It was supposed to be two hours of 'rest', but the time was utilised for activities that would bond the boys for life. With practically no supervision, small groups of friends-in-the-making played games, strolled into the bushes searching for berries and rolled down the green slopes frolicking in the hot sun. It was fun-time, a time that every student remembers with clarity.

After the games period in the evening, the tired boys came back to their living area only to get ready for homework. Since there was no place in the congested rooms for desks, they had to dress for dinner and head towards their classrooms where the prefects and monitors would supervise them. Of course comics were hidden inside textbooks, letters written and mischief made during this time, especially when there was no exam pressure. Some tired souls just slept through this study time only to be punished by the prefects.

With the smell of freshly made sambaar and rice wafting around, the siren would announce dinner, and the boys would head to the mess.

Punishment was an integral part of training at the school and later at the NDA and Air Force Academy. Punishment was generally of two types—physical and mental, and official and unofficial. Mental punishment included just standing in a corner or hearing a long-drawn ML (moral lecture) from the senior or being marched before the duty masters when things got out of hand. Although corporal punishment was a strict no-no, some seniors resorted to it to get the juniors in line. That slap, pinch or twist of the arm would be better than the cane. Some other 'official' punishments that the seniors could give the juniors were to make them run, front-roll, side-roll or simply jump up and down.

In one of his essays on his schooldays, MP mentions the first time he decided to bunk school and go and watch a very popular orchestra in the nearby town. The temporary absence of their dreaded housemaster made many boys, including MP, muster the courage. While the loud music was being enjoyed by a large number of students bunking en masse, word got around that the headmaster had decided to have a special 'fall-in' (headcount) that evening.

A wave of panic ran through the crowd, to the surprise of the performing artistes and other spectators, and a melee broke out as a whole lot of 'bunkers' ran out of the venue towards the woods that took them back to school through a 'secret' route. On getting into his bed panting after his midnight dash, MP was almost sure he had escaped detection. When he was told by the prefect a little while later that the headmaster had come and checked out the dorm and taken the missing names on a chit of paper, MP almost fainted with fear. His first-ever bunk had turned into a nightmare. He tossed and turned through the night wondering what was to happen to him.

The next morning the whole gang stood in the headmaster's office trying to explain where they were by spinning stories that did nothing to impress the angry man. Since it was a case of mass indiscipline, it was decided that all parents would be informed in writing about the misdemeanour of their children. Being mortally scared of his Acchan who was a strict disciplinarian, Anil dreaded going home for the Christmas vacation.

To MP's relief, Acchan made no mention of the escapade right through his stay. 'Maybe the postal department goofed up', MP thought. Quoting from his diary, 'As I was packing my bags to get back to school, my father walked in, and to my utter disbelief, just taunted me for getting caught... "Son! Smarten up!" was his succinct fatherly counsel. That is when I realised there is an 11th commandment—"thou shalt not be found out!"'

MP also writes about the time he was caned for not using the mosquito net at night. Sleeping without one was forbidden, but MP would feel claustrophobic in such an enclosed space and decided to disobey. The resulting caning would leave welts on his calves and thighs that would take time to heal.

It was difficult to hide the welts when he went home on leave. The usual shorts were abandoned and replaced by the mundu (wraparound/lungi). His parents thought it strange but took it as a sign of his coming of age! He writes, 'My brother found out why I was keeping my legs covered and wanted to go and sneak to Amma and Acchan; he had to be bribed sufficiently to keep his mouth shut!'

Another incident that landed MP in trouble was when he had a skirmish with his friend and dorm neighbour B Ramesh. Acchan had just come over on Sunday and handed over a small packet of Cadbury's Gems to MP. MP decided not to share the goodies and to consume them little by little after lights out. Around midnight, MP was awakened by the sound of Ramesh munching on his packet of chocolate. A small scuffle later, MP managed to partially recover the candy.

The housemaster, AKG, got wind of the fight over food. 'Someone who didn't get the booty squealed', writes MP. Both got a good walloping. When Acchan came to pick him up for the Onam vacation a few days later, George Sir told him about the fight. 'Extremely upset about the whole episode, Acchan never brought eatables to the school for a long time after', MP writes.

EACH OF the dorms that housed the 5th and 6th class children had a matron. Sarojini Amma was the one who looked after MP and his friends in the junior house hostel. She was the only mother figure available to look after the little fellows in the early years. In the first few days of school, she went from bed to bed to check if the boys were crying themselves to sleep. With soothing words and some folklore, she managed to distract them. She was there to sew on buttons lost during skirmishes, make them kanji (starchy water from boiled rice) when they were sick and administer home remedies for common ailments. She knew each boy under her charge almost as well as a mother would and was deeply involved in their development from boys to men.

There was a small area between the living quarters and the washrooms which was used for drying clothes. After the bath, the boys lined up for what was called the 'kuli' parade, an inspection by the matron. Amma sat perched on a stool on the veranda and checked armpits, knees, nails and ears for dirt and grime one by one. Next the boys had to display their freshly washed underwear, socks and handkerchiefs, all hung on outstretched arms for scrutiny. The defaulters would be sent back for an encore!

Twice a week Amma supervised what was called the dhobi clothes event. A team was formed to count and account for each type of clothing being sent to the dhobi. One boy counted the shorts while the other was in charge of the shirts while still another had to look after a pile of towels and suchlike. This turned out to be quite a chaotic event with Amma howling at everyone to be attentive and maintain discipline, explains an old boy.

As the children sat down to eat in the mess, Amma would go from table to table to check if all the vegetables were being eaten, often telling them of the health benefits of each, though no one was really interested. She also ensured that proper hygiene was followed in the mess—washing of hands before and after meals was enforced strictly, much to the annoyance of the boys. So involved was she that she would forget that she had a small daughter waiting at home for her. 'Go and check on my daughter Maya', she would often say to one of the boys. 'See if she has had her glass of milk or not.'

She had noticed that MP was a quiet boy and often spoke to him when she could find him alone. MP remembered her often when we talked about our youth. She had been the one who had helped wean him away from his mother. Although the children moved out of Sarojini Amma's care when they went on to class 7, MP remembered her contribution in his growing up years fondly.

'Sarojini Amma was a perfect antidote to the strict, cane-wielding housemaster!' he once told me.

SD Princ, a classmate of MP, says, 'Sarojini Amma had to deal with each child differently when they arrived at school. She realised that besides their varying upbringing and financial background, they also had to cross the language barrier'. Even for the boys who came from different parts of Kerala, accents and dialects differed. It was more difficult for boys who came from different States like Bihar, West Bengal and Haryana to understand the language and settle in.

'Even English words of everyday use like "bathroom" were alien to the boys', says Princ. 'After a few days, a new "school language" developed and the boys were able to understand each other better. Those from outside the State were also able to get by with a smattering of Malayalam in a few days.' With this hurdle crossed, the bonds between the young ones grew stronger.

MP never lost his Chirayinkeezhu accent, says Princ. The moment he got back home, even in his later years, the first thing he did was shed his 'city attire' and don the mundu and vest to blend with the rest. With his physical transformation complete, his acquired accent would change back to the chaste Malayalam spoken at home, indicating the love for his roots, remembers Princ. He became one with the village, attending all functions, celebrations, street plays and musicals with enthusiasm, making everyone feel that he had not gone out of their lives at all.

THE SCHOOL offered many avenues for toughening up mentally and physically. There were 11 football grounds, eight hockey grounds, adequate plinths for volleyball and basketball and, of course, the 'obstacle course' on campus. Games were compulsory and the cadet was helped to hone his skills in the game in which he showed most promise.

Each house had to compete with the other in games, academics and other extracurricular activities for what was called the Cock House trophy, awarded to the best overall house. The events were fiercely competitive and the boys learnt the basics of team spirit, group dynamics and team goals above personal ones. These values stayed with them throughout life, the boys remember.

MP writes a beautiful essay about a cricket match played with a sister school in Trivandrum. Although he underplays his own contribution, he brings out clearly the fierce competition and the strategising. 'In my 11th, we had a cliffhanger of an interschool final versus Loyola', MP writes. 'They made about

170. Chasing, we were down to six for 18, their bowler Sabu Rajan claiming all six. I joined my captain Nandu and kept blocking and taking singles.' Eventually, Nandu smashed a century and MP carried his bat, remaining not out on 22, their team falling short by just two runs!

In another match with the same school the next year, MP and his friends learned the art of feigning a misfield, running out the batsman when he attempted to take a run with a direct throw. They put a lot of practice into the feigning, and also into knocking the stumps off with sharp flat throws from the deep. The first three wickets fell to MP's throws, and the Loyola coach frantically indicated to the batsmen in the middle that no one was to run when the ball went in his direction! MP writes, 'Loyola lost nine wickets, seven run-outs! Chasing, we lost that match again by a narrow margin. I, the premier batsman, played a silly shot to get out. Still regret my silly shot...'

In an article published on *rediff.com* he writes, 'I started playing cricket in my alma mater, Sainik School Kazhakootam, and wore the school colours for two years. I was so passionate about cricket that despite the crammed day in the NDA and IAF, I would somehow steal morsels of the telecast or radio commentary to keep track of every match India played'. During my visits to him at the paraplegic home many years later, MP would often surprise me with an absolute knowledge of every game being played and the achievements of the cricketing greats of those times.

He reminisced, 'I still remember slithering out of the comfort of my sleeping bag at 0430 hours in sub-10-degree temperatures in Leh to watch the first ball being bowled in an ODI between

India and New Zealand played at Launceston (Tasmania) in February 1986. Many colleagues gave me up as a loony when I spent a good part of two days watching Mudassar Nazar and Quasim Omar plod, plod and plod, in one of the most boring matches in test history—India vs Pakistan, second test at Faisalabad, October 1984'.

Although the school teams were the domain of the seniors, ie the 12th standard, MP represented three school teams whilst in the 11th itself, the most difficult being selection for the football team. In the 12th grade his hockey coach selected him as the school hockey captain, but MP proposed his friend Sasidharan's name instead since he had already been selected for the NDA by then. In one of his mails to a friend, Ganga Devi, he writes, 'In Trivandrum, I've played in all three stadiums—Central, Chandrashekaran Nair, University, plus GV Raja Sports School. Aah, those were the days...'

MP idolised many cricketers, but Richard Hadlee most of all. MP was so mesmerised by Hadlee's bowling action and swing that he started to ape him. Having perfected the run-up and delivery stride, he and G Prakash, schoolmate and later NDA course-mate, practised for hours in the heat and grime, using tattered old balls discarded by the PT sir. MP then strategised how not to get out to a 'Hadlee delivery'. He realised that if he modified his stance to a more 'square on' one, his reactions to ward off the ball with the bat would be that much better. Prakash explains, 'While it became extremely difficult to get the chap out, it also meant that he was restricted in his stroke play and could not score many runs'. He continued to egg MP on to adopt this stance, secretly knowing that it would be good for his own team which was in serious competition with Anil's!

There were a number of innovative games that the boys invented. One such was 'soks' ball cricket. Old socks and lost socks were rolled over each other to make a soft ball. The bat could be any vertical equipment including a hockey stick. These were keenly contested games within the confines of the dormitories. MP's batchmates remember his prowess both in the indoor and outdoor version of the game with pride.

Another game was modified carrom. The rectangular tin cover of the sewing kit served as the playing board while the small buttons were the 'carroms' and a large-sized button the striker. The game would be watched by spectators who would bet on the outcome—not money but toffees and small treasures like photographs of stars.

R Radhish, a serving IAF officer and a close friend of MP, remembers one game that ended in disaster. 'We had just finished our tea with the famed Carborandum (the school bakery produced a biscuit so hard that it had to be soaked in tea to be eaten!) and were walking past a tree with a very low branch that could be swung on. We decided to invent an impromptu long jump game. The one who could jump from the farthest point and catch hold of the branch and swing on it would be the winner.'

The game started well enough and the difficulty levels kept mounting. In one of the jumps, Radhish took off, held on to the branch but the momentum got the better of him. Trying to break his fall with his arms, he realised that he had bent one of his arms at a grotesque angle and was in excruciating pain. MP ran up to him immediately, helped him get the arm straightened out, and took him to the prefect. They both decided to claim that the fall had occurred in the bathroom. Radhish was soon seen in a plaster, enjoying all the 'shamming' and restful days in a sling. 'A lot of tales had to be spun later to hide the first lie, especially to parents and well-wishers.' Radhish reminisces that it would have been better if they had stuck to the truth—a lesson he followed later in life.

The infirmary was the place to be if you wanted a break from the taxing routine. The boys believed that the infirmary only had Iodex and some horrible tasting 'mixture' in large brown bottles that was used for every ailment. If you wanted to feign a fever, all you had to do was to put a slice of onion under the armpit for a few hours. It would stink but the temperature would surely go up by a couple of degrees and you would be grounded for a few days. The boys would sham an eye infection by putting some tobacco (obtained from a beedi or cigarette butt thrown carelessly around by some staff) into their eyes. It was painful, but made the eye sufficiently red and watery. Besides all these, the most common ailment was 'tomak ek' (stomach ache) or a headache which got you respite from PT or parade for a day or two.

Prakash also describes the making of the 'Colgate Calendar'. A window was cut into the rectangular stiff paper cover of a toothpaste tube. A spindle with a roll of paper with numbers written on it was ensconced within. The rotation of the spindle displayed the all-important number in the window—the number of days left for the next vacation. Interestingly, this practice continues at NDA where 'DLTGH' (Days Left To Go Home) is marked in bold letters in one corner of the blackboard in each classroom.

THE BOYS were perpetually hungry since they were growing up fast and expending their energies faster. In the 1970s, with Rs 2.50 as the total amount of ration authorised by the government per cadet, it was difficult to provide wholesome and nutritious meals to the children. The school had to innovate and set up its own bakery, piggery, poultry and small farm to augment the rations. All this and the dedication of the cooks and waiters ensured that the cadets got their fill.

But the stomach had its demands and its pangs had to be assuaged. The boys were soon expert at climbing trees, tearing the top layers off the coconuts and getting to the business end of the fruit. They would also eat the cashew fruit. Tapioca, however, could not be eaten raw. The root was pulled out of the earth, washed and scraped with a used shaving blade. Then it had to be boiled and garnished before it could be eaten. MP told me how it was done. A heater was made of two shoe-polish cans separated by a piece of glass and tied together with string. Each can was attached to a wire and connected to an electric socket, turning the contraption into a rather dangerous water heater. As the water boiled in mugs, the tapioca would be added along with salt and red chili powder spirited away from the dining hall. Finally, a dash of coconut hair oil went in to get the 'fried' effect. The whole concoction would be a gooey but tasty mixture—a taste still remembered by many old boys.

Sundays were free days and the boys explored the nooks and crannies of the campus. There were meadows to roll in, ponds to be inspected for water snakes, frogs and a variety of insects, secret pathways to be found through the grounds.

On this day came parents, relatives and friends in hordes. Any relative, friend, villager and even baby in arms who came to the school was referred to as the 'Parent' pronounced 'paa-rent'. With parents came goodies. MP recalled that the parcels came in various shapes and sizes. The city people brought cakes, chocolates and the like, while those from the nearby villages got the *acchappams*, *unniyappams, sukhiyan, ethakka appam* and fruit.

On the school annual day parents and relatives turned up in large numbers and the school bore a colourful and sprightly look. After the trophies and prizes were given away, there was an entertainment programme and the day culminated in a dinner for all the guests. Sheeja writes, 'Probably the largest crowd that attended the school anniversary was from Chirayinkeezhu. Our group used to come back and discuss the occasion for weeks. Those were the days!'

ONCE, AS some boys returned from a late night show, they saw the master's office lights on. Worried, they slipped into their beds pretending to be asleep. The master walked in and 'woke' them up. The scared faces looked at him expecting a volley of expletives and the award of punishment.

But the master turned to them and said, 'You boys must have missed your dinner for the movie... I hope you have eaten something. If you are hungry, I will ask my wife to cook up a quick snack'. Stunned, the boys just nodded. Saying goodnight, the master nonchalantly walked out of the room with the boys staring at each other in disbelief.

Of this masterstroke MP writes, 'KMN (the master) dealt with the situation with impeccable sagacity, grace and gentleness. Hats off to him for defusing a sticky situation with utmost aplomb and astuteness'. The master managed to instill self-discipline without upbraiding them or wielding the cane, he adds, ensuring that those boys never bunked again.

Another old boy describes how some of them would dress up in mundus and set off to town with a towel wrapped around their heads much as the local villagers did. Four coconuts felled from a tree would be carried on their heads, fetching them about a rupee when sold to the local merchant, who actually fleeced the boys and sold the coconuts at a hundred per cent profit.

But that one rupee was enough to buy a 'floor ticket' at a local movie theatre. This meant sitting on the floor so close to the screen that they had to move their heads to follow the performer from one edge of the screen to the other! But it was worth it. 'It was as if we could touch our iconic stars on the screen', says an old boy. Entertainment over, the next activity was finding food. The 40 paisa left over was not enough. The 40 paisa had to be turned into a rupee again.

From the local *paan* shop, the 40 paisa was changed for eight coins of 5 paisa each. These were used to bet on an 'under seven-over seven' game on the roadside. If one managed to win a few more coins by betting correctly, it was treat time. For a rupee, one could buy four parottas (pan fried roti) and beef curry (with hardly any beef) followed by a cup of sweet tea and a cigarette shared between those who dared to smoke.

Prem Nazir, the legendary Malayalam actor, was MP's hero in those days. He held the world record for playing the lead in 725 films and was regarded as the most successful actor in Indian cinema. Besides his movies which were not to be missed, there were the Sridevi-Kamal Haasan starrers, which were very popular in those times.

There was a movie show every week at the school. A rickety old 16 mm projector was set up adjacent to the building and the movie screened on the wall as soon as it got dark. MP remembers that preparations for the movie began well after evening tea when the juniors were made to carry the heavy iron chairs—called 'iron' by the children—to the venue for the seniors and teachers to sit. The show itself was punctuated with frequent breakdowns of the projector, the sound system or the reel itself.

Prem Nazir was a resident of Chirayinkeezhu and lived close to MP's home. So besotted was he by the actor that MP made it a point to read as much as he could about him and also find time to go and see him in person as and when he visited the village. Returning from leave, while everyone told stories of the movies and other fun they had had, MP told them 'live' Nazir stories. He, in fact, became a repository of information on the great legend and as a tribute to both Nazir and MP, Sheeja wrote the Prem Nazir biography in Malayalam which has just been released.

THERE WERE three breaks in a year: one long summer vacation and two short stints for Onam and Christmas. At Chirayinkeezhu, the whole village waited for the young lad to come home. How much MP had changed became a topic for the evening gossip.

The home would be spruced up for the arrival. Acchan often joked with Amma that it was Onam time everytime the lad was home. The best of sweets would be prepared in advance, fresh fish would be bought and prepared in various styles, pickles readied and the rooms cleaned out. 'Even if our schools closed earlier than the Sainik School, our real holidays began when Anil arrived home', writes Sheeja. 'The attachment between Anil and I was "wordless"', she adds. As they had a short time to spend together, there was an unwritten policy between brother and sister that wherever MP went Sheeja went too, and vice versa. This was how Sheeja was able to pick up a number of field games like hockey and volleyball. She claims that this training alongside MP and his friends made her bolder and more confident in taking on the trials and tribulations of life.

Amma was one of the best cooks in the village, with a large kitchen and a larger heart. She cooked for many of the old, poor and needy, and was well-known for her festive specialties. MP remembered that no one ever went back hungry. If there was no food at hand she would quickly cook some rice with salt and condiments and serve it hot. MP's heart swelled with pride when he saw Amma do this.

Although he was happy to be home, Sheeja remembers that it would be some time before MP would get out of his shell and start enjoying the holiday. There was lots to be done and little time. She told me that MP carried his school bag home and often was seen smelling it when he missed school during these vacations.

MP had always been an animal lover. As a small boy, Amma remembers him picking up a cat or dog from the streets and bringing it home for company. He would spend a lot of time talking to them and disciplining them. When he went back to school these poor animals were out of the home and back on the streets, thanks to Acchan!

Once MP was very angry with his pet hen who he lovingly called 'Toppi-khozi' or 'the hen with a cap' since she had a nice little red plume on her head. The hen was pecking away in the corners of the home while her chicks wandered all over looking for her. 'This is not right', thought the boy. 'The mother needs to be disciplined; she can't shirk her responsibility of looking after her young ones.'

He ran all over the courtyard after the clucking hen, managed to corner her and gave her a good whack on her back. The boy did not estimate the power of his stroke and the poor bird collapsed and died! A shocked MP collected the dead bird in his arms, and went to Sheeja crying aloud. Sheeja also burst into tears and they went sobbing to Amma. Amma remembers that it took quite a while for MP to cope with the shock of killing the bird.

Sheeja recollects that one of their neighbours, an old man, saw Anil crying and consoled him. He said, 'Shame, shame, aren't you going to be a soldier? A soldier never cries! He must be courageous!' The tears were quickly wiped away.

From the streets of Chirayinkeezhu, MP's friend Indrabalan picked up a pup and gifted it to MP. It was promptly named Tingu. Mani the cat came home in similar circumstances and both became permanent members of their home over the years. Indrabalan, Sheeja remembers, joined MP at the Sainik School later. Over the years, MP asked about his pets in every letter that he wrote from school and later from NDA and the paraplegic home: 'How is Mani's tail? She had a scratch at the tip; has it healed? I hope she is not losing her hair now. Please don't give sweets to Tingu...it is not good for him.' 'He treated them like humans', remembers Sheeja. Acchan didn't like pets inside the home but seeing MP's love for the animals, relented in time. Both the pets had their favourite part of MP's bed to sleep in, Sheeja says. Tingu and Mani lived for many years after the accident and their presence at home reminded everyone of Anil.

Often during his leave, MP would hire a cycle to go visiting relatives in nearby villages. All of them wanted to see the bright young lad and Amma advised him to go and meet them at least once on every trip. Sheeja would feel left out since she was not allowed to go along; she loved being in her brother's company and emulated him in many ways. The moment I came face to face with her for the first time, it was as if MP was right in front of me! She was, and remains, fiercely possessive of her brother.

Sometimes, Sheeja said, MP would be jealous of her, but didn't know how to react. Acchan would have her on his lap while he read his morning paper sitting on the big swing fitted in the doorway, treating her to small sips of coffee from his steel glass. MP would watch from afar and gesture with his eyes that she should get off. Sheeja would make faces at him and dare him. She explains that MP also wanted attention from his father but could not get himself to tell him so or get too close physically to him. 'It was a typical "Kerala" father-son relationship based on awe and high respect', explains Sheeja. It was considered 'girlish' for boys to show such emotion. 'Each time he left home after leave, he would cry silently in his room before he emerged stoic and calm in front of everyone.'

When she was told that Anil kept sobbing even in a coma just three days before he died, Sheeja thought, 'Maybe these were the same tears as when he was leaving home...'

FOR ALL his outdoor activities and escapades, MP did find time to study hard too. His affinity for knowledge was such that he soon became the blue-eyed boy of his teachers. But he was always ready to challenge the system. Princ, a former journalist turned PRO, recalls that in the early years the students had to write a page of English and Hindi everyday from their textbook to hone their language and writing skills. MP was convinced that his Hindi teacher would not even check what was written and decided to prove it to his friends. Instead of the page prescribed by the teacher, he wrote mockingly of the terrible condition of the master's scooter. If he was caught, there would be severe repercussions. They waited with bated breath but sure enough, MP's notebook came back with a large red tick mark across the page!

Princ says, 'MP came from a completely rural background. One saw the extra effort and energy he had to put in to catch up with those who were ahead of him in academics. By class 6, MP had worked his way amongst the top of his class'.

There is a beautiful account by MP about a bicycle hike to Kovalam, the seaside resort located just 20 km from the school. Fifteen classmates were selected. MP was extremely excited about the trip. Bicycles were hired and allotted. MP took a test ride and proceeded to adjust the brakes, tighten the chain, pad the warped seat with some cloth and check the bell a number of times. Then he rode proudly around the campus showing off his beauty before giving it a final wash and polish the night before the journey.

'A flush of frisson gripped me. Excitement coursed through my veins. I barely slept. Early morning, I went out and ran my fingers up and down my cycle, as though it were the neck of a thoroughbred that I was to mount at the races that day', he writes. The bikes were parked on the beautiful sandy beach and the boys ran towards the sea under the watchful eyes of their young math teacher Mani, who had recently joined the school.

Off flew their shirts, socks and shoes and MP was soon frolicking with his friends in the shallow waters. Before long, the adept swimmers were emboldened to venture into deeper waters and MP was unhappy that he couldn't because he had never learnt to swim. 'I chastised myself for being a non-swimmer and missing out on the fun', writes MP. 'Boredom set in and incited me to turn adventurous. With lemming-like lunacy, I incrementally tiptoed into deeper water. As I admired my own spunk, a whopping wave whacked me; I lost my footing and capsized.' He went under, sputtering and flailing his arms and legs in panic. He managed to surface for a lungful of air and then went under again, gasping. Luckily he was seen by one of his friends and rescued. He lay on the warm sand coughing and spewing salty seawater.

Anil continues, 'Chastened, spitting seawater, I trudged onwards with my tail firmly between my legs. I vowed to learn swimming then'.

Right through school, MP did not display any real affinity for leadership. He would prefer to observe from the background, gain as much knowledge as he could, but at the end of the day, go with the flow. That was until leadership was literally thrust upon him.

In Class 11, MP was made a school prefect. 'He understood his responsibilities well but never got down to punishing any of his juniors', muses Princ. He jokes that MP preferred to remain quiet and lead from the back!

The lure of flying

THE INDIAN Air Force had presented a Harward aircraft to the school soon after it was established. It was bright yellow and stood strategically in front of the academic block. MP writes that he found the kite irresistible the moment he saw it. He often clambered into the cockpit and moved the control column that shifted the controls in squeaky movements. As he got bolder, he tried to yank the propeller to see if it moved but it was jammed tight. All through his years at school, he spent much of his free time leaning against the nacelle of the aircraft, dreaming and thinking about the science of flying. 'One day', he thought to himself, 'I will zoom into the skies and fight the enemies'. 'I wanted to defy gravity, to soar and swoop like an eagle', he writes. Once he had his sights clear, the only thing left was to stay focused on joining the IAF through the NDA at the first opportunity.

MP appeared for the 64th course at NDA whilst he was in class 11, but unfortunately did not make it in the fiercely competitive exam. This failure was a wake-up call for him—it was time to get serious. Only two more chances remained and the 12th standard board exams loomed large. With no time for tomfoolery, MP dived into his books and managed to pass the entrance exam for the 65th course commencing at NDA at the beginning of 1981. Now he had to concentrate on his selection rather than prepare for his 12th standard exams as the others did.

For his selection interview he proceeded to the Air Force Selection Board at Mysore and was allotted Chest No 1 during the selection process, indicating that he was still one of the youngest of the participants. Having passed the five-day interview process, MP was soon undergoing some tough medical tests at Bangalore to join the flying branch of the air force. As he went through his last six months in school, a confident and excited MP Anil Kumar awaited the merit list and call-up letter.Just a handful of them were heading to NDA whilst the rest were contemplating college and other avenues in the civvy street. MP was pretty confident of making it to the final merit list and therefore decided to take it easy. The all-important board exams were for lesser mortals, he claimed now!

Prakash remembers how they used to go to town almost every second day to check for the NDA merit list while the rest of the class broke their backs studying. This was, however, just a ploy to get out of school. *Sankarabharanam*, the 1979 classic, had just been released. Prakash wanted to learn the movie's songs (by KV Mahadeven) by heart and the only way to do it was to see the movie as many times as possible! MP loved musical dramas and doted on the actresses Tulasi Shivamani and Manju Bhargavi.

THUS, NINE years at the Sainik School readied a simple village boy for the real world and real military training.

It taught him to start thinking independently, to stride into the unknown fearlessly and to look at life as an adventure. It also taught him to adapt to any environment. There were no more barriers of language, food, accent, clothes, caste, creed or religion. The boys now believed they were all equal and developed a healthy respect for each other. The strong bonding that develops at school remains for life. The value of good friendship and the ability to discern that group goals are more important than personal ones were understood at school. A fierce but healthy sense of competition was also developed. Spirit also made MP more compassionate, and he went out of his way to help anyone who asked for it.

Cherian, an old school boy writes, 'Ninety or so of us were put into this crucible called school for an experiment. I feel that the gamble, to a large extent, has paid off'. So many of the schoolmates—seniors and juniors—have excelled in their chosen fields and someone or the other is always around for help anywhere in the world. He adds, 'I believe that the years spent at school, baptised by fire as Prem C Nair used to call it, had an effect on our character and psyche, and helped us make a positive contribution to society at large'.

MP says in one of his articles, 'I decided to extrapolate the common thread in the fabric of our lives at school. Why is it that I remember incidents that happened so long long ago with vivid detail? Perhaps that is the pull of the school'. Removed from the cocoon of their homes at such an early age, the bonds forged of shared experiences in a magical place possibly compensated for parental attention, he concludes.

In his tribute to the school, Prakash writes, 'Masters, as we called them, were actually masters of our destinies. They were not Dronacharyas who tutored one Arjuna to win a Kurukshetra, but trained an army of soldiers to fight many of life's battles. They were not Aristotles who conferred philosophy to the greatest conqueror, but administered collective wisdom to a generation of men. They were not Chanakyas, to whisper political intrigue in the ears of a Chandragupta, but shared insightful thoughts with hundreds of aspiring minds. They were not Hardys who fostered a great Ramanujan under his wing, but kindled the flame of knowledge in all their wards. They left a lasting influence, ever so subtle, in every act, action or activity throughout our lives. We owe it to them for what we are today'.

With a hint of a moustache, little pimples appearing on his face and standing at five-and-a-half feet, MP was now ready to join the NDA. He was academically and physically equipped to take on the trials and tribulations of training for the next three years.

Making of the military man

1945. THE Second World War was just over and most of the world, including India, was coming to terms with the enormous losses suffered. In the next two years India went through a tumultuous independence from 200 years of British rule. While the leadership of the country got busy drafting the Constitution and charting the future of the democracy, economy, education and health services, senior military and civilian leaders focused on developing a motivated and organised defence force. There was an urgent need to replace British military leadership with our own military leaders. Thus was born the concept of establishing a 'War Academy' to produce military leaders trained in a tri-services environment. This academy was first established in mid-1948, christened the Inter Services Wing, and later the Joint Services Wing (JSW). The first course passed out of this institution in January 1949.

The JSW was designed along the lines of the prestigious West Point Academy of the United States. The JSW grew and prospered at the military barracks in Clement Town in Dehradun, with a mix of officers from all three services and a major chunk of trainers from the British army to begin with.

It was soon decided to shift the institution to the sprawling 8,022-acre campus near Khadakwasla in Pune, pledged by Morarji Desai, then Chief Minister of the State of Bombay. The foundation stone was laid by Prime Minister Jawaharlal Nehru in January 1949. The JSW finally shifted to Pune as the National Defence Academy in 1955, with a formal inauguration on January 16. The motto of the academy was, and has been, *to train and develop future military leaders to possess the requisite qualities of leadership, integrity, character and intellect through broad-based military, physical and academic education*.

The NDA grew and prospered over the years, its alumni doing it proud in the wars that were fought in 1962, 1965, 1971 and the Kargil conflict of 1999. Apart from being leaders of men, the alumni have proved to be great mountaineers, cosmonauts, sportsmen, researchers, creative writers, artists, corporate honchos and Olympic champions.

NDA is located in the tranquil and pristine hills of the Western Ghats and the large area it occupies serves to train cadets of all three services. At one end is Khadakwasla Lake, which is used for naval training and water sports, while at the other end is a full-fledged airfield where the air force cadets train. In between are hills and jungles, ideal terrain for the training of the green berets or 'pongos' as we affectionately termed our army counterparts. The majestic Sudan Block is at the heart of NDA: it houses the main administrative offices and also the arts academic block. The Science Block is another large building though not as grand as Sudan Block and here are located the science faculty and allied laboratories. A large parade ground, named the Arun Khetrapal parade ground after the legendary Armoured Corps officer who won the Param Vir Chakra for his valour in the 1971 war, is almost 800 metres long, with a high ship mast at the entrance and located right in front of the Science Block.

The academy reflects a tri-services environment. Sudan Block is shaped like a huge artillery gun while the other buildings look like ships and aeroplanes when viewed from the air. Even the organisation of the cadets into divisions, squadrons and battalions is on the lines of the navy, air force and army respectively. The NDA cadet wears a khaki uniform, with a tri-services maroon emblem on the shoulder that is symbolic of the mixing of the green, white and blue of the three services with an equal measure of blood.

Sudan Block was funded by the 100,000 pounds gifted by the government of Sudan in 1941 in gratitude for the sacrifices of Indian troops who defended Sudan in the Second World War. Writing about Sudan Block in the school journal released on the 25th anniversary of his passing out, Anil says, 'I have often gaped at the Sudan, not to admire its architectural splendour but to suss out how PP Davis, two years my senior, scaled its gigantic dome disregarding the hazards'. His reference was to the two cadets who became legends at NDA for their escapade. They dodged a sentry, hid their footwear and unscrewed the padlock of the stairwell leading up to the steps of the dome which led to the summit from the outside. To help Davis reach the apex of the dome, his buddy Bipin Bakshi had to lift Davis on his shoulders. He proceeded to tie a hanky around the lightening conductor and the duo slunk back to their rooms in the darkness, awaiting the flutter it would cause the next day.

To their disappointment, nobody seemed to notice the small hanky fluttering in the wind above the massive dome. They decided to repeat the performance the next night, this time positioning a riding pith-hat atop the dome. A Soviet General was visiting the academy the next day, conducted by the Commandant. Admiring the grandeur of the Sudan Block from afar, he noticed the pith-hat with the hanky fluttering beneath it. He asked, 'Shto e'ta (what's that)?' The Commandant, taken aback, gathered his wits and replied, 'Err...ahh...that is an exotic bird's nest!' The bewildered General exclaimed, '*Khorosho, khorosho, o'ochin priyatna!* (Good, good, that's lovely!)'

MP adds, 'Though the General was impressed, the Commandant was not amused by the caper'. In fact, he was livid. Soon, all 1,500 cadets of the academy were being 'sorted out' by a set of instructors and drill ustaads. The boys took the collective punishment in good spirit and the story became part of NDA folklore.

The academy boasts excellant infrastructure for games and sports, and almost all sports and leisure activities are available to the cadet. Bombay Stadium hosts games like cricket and athletics while there are numerous football, hockey, volleyball and basketball fields all over the campus. Two Olympic-size swimming pools cater to water sports. A large number of clubs offer co-curricular activities, from trekking, aero-modelling and stargazing to painting and dramatics.

Since the academy is so vast, the bicycle is the primary

form of mobility, the cycle an integral part of the 'kit' issued to the cadet when he joins the academy. Whether the cycle is serviceable or not, it has to be carried everywhere and often one would find cadets running with their bikes alongside from one class to another. The bike is also carried as a 'garland' around the neck occasionally, when a senior wants to correct his junior for minor infringements!

In 1981, when MP joined, the academy was divided into 12 'squadrons', numbered from 'A' (Alpha) to 'L' (Lima). Each squadron had a mix of boys from the 2nd to 6th term living under one roof, distributed in four divisions. Akin to the 'House' in school, these squadrons compete against each other in all disciplines to win the Champion Squadron banner, one of the most coveted collective awards on campus. The Champion Squadron is privileged to hoist the Champion Squadron banner atop their squadron building, its cadets wearing their lanyards on the right shoulder instead of the left, and the squadron standing first in every parade for that term.

Where then, were the first-termers? The freshers reported to a place called NDA Wing, Ghorpuri, located at the other end of Pune. This was a small campus compared to the NDA, catering only to one course of 300 cadets. This is where each batch spent its first six months. The separate campus allowed the freshmen to be cocooned from seniors during the initial part of their training, helping the 'course' to bond before they were distributed amongst the 12 squadrons in the second term. Moreover, it increased the capacity of the academy by 300-odd cadets without additional infrastructure required at the main campus. The separate campus was maintained for just a few years. As the physical capacity of the NDA increased, the NDA Wing was closed down and the first-term cadets started reporting to the main campus at Khadakwasla.

MP writes, 'The cadets at NDA are a microcosmic representation of India. The academy's fundamental objective therefore is to weave this heterogeneous collection into an organic whole with Indianness as its soul...The NDA is a true crucible of the manifold constituents that make this great nation, where sub-identities are coalesced to yield a national identity. Though we hailed from diverse backgrounds, spoke multiple tongues, we never judged anyone by his religion, caste, creed, parentage or such pigeonholes'.

The campus at Ghorpuri was rudimentary to say the least and located in old dilapidated army barracks. The 288 cadets of the 65th Course reported here between January and February 1981 and training began in earnest in February. Six more boys from the previous course (who were relegated) were appointed to direct the rookies. The first thing on the agenda on arrival was a haircut. The barbers waited gleefully with their shears and a long line of boys waited to be cut to size! At the end of 10 minutes, each boy emerged with a crewcut that might have made it difficult even for parents to identify the son they had left at the academy a few hours ago!

The boys were issued their kit and measured for some of the ceremonial uniforms that would be issued subsequently. They were given their NDA roll numbers which, like the numbers at Sainik School, would remain synonymous with their names for the rest of their lives. For ease of administration and some healthy competition, the boys were distributed into two squadrons

M (Mike) and N (November). The odd numbers, including MP (14823), went to N squadron and the even numbers like mine (15046) to M.

For the first six months, the course-mates competed fiercely to win the overall best squadron trophy. MP describes, for instance, the selection of the basketball teams. One evening, Captain PS Nijjar, who was one of the divisional officers (DivOs in short), asked the group, 'Who has represented basketball in school?' A large number of hands went up. He walked around as if in deep thought, 'Who has represented basketball at the national level?' A dozen or so hands again went up. They were asked to fallout and stand separately. True to form, Captain Nijjar hailed the senior cadet and ordered, 'Cadet Jhala! Take these boys for boxing'. It was the first of many such anecdotes packed with military humour. The anecdotes are similar across time despite the fact that most of us would like to say, 'The academy was so different when we were there!'

My father, an armyman himself, came to drop me at the academy with my trunk et al. As I was walking to the reception, the adjutant, Captain AS Rao, walked in to direct the process, barking out his orders in a nasal tone. My father immediately recognised Rao as one of his pupils when he'd served as an instructor at the Indian Military Academy (IMA). After much backslapping, Captain Rao turned around and asked my father, 'Your boy, sir?' 'Yes', said my father proudly, 'Now he is yours, sort him out!' And sort me out he did. The moment my father left, I was getting my first lessons in rolling and frog-jumping!

The first few days at the NDA Wing are used by the divisional officers to 'sort out' the boys, eradicating all traces of civilian behaviour. No 'Yah' or 'Yeah', we were taught to say 'Yes, Sir' in so many punishing ways that 'Yes, Sir' became a habit! Time management and timeliness were drilled into us in every conceivable way. It was incumbent on us to reach the required place in time and congregate in threes in neat rows and files. No activity would begin till the 'report' was given. Having completed the headcount, the senior-most would bring them all to attention, proceed to the officer and shout out the report. If anyone moved, the whole procedure would be repeated till such time the DivO was satisfied. Once the report was accepted by him, a go-ahead would be given for the activity to commence.

This was true for games, PT, parade and even meals! Even a minute's delay was unacceptable and would lead to collective punishment. There were a few in the course who were a little wayward and since they did not fall in line, the entire lot of us had to suffer unnecessary punishment. These guys were then sorted out by us course-mates and they learnt to behave and follow the rules.

It was the first weekend of February and pretty chilly. The course was looking forward to a well-earned Sunday break. Soon after dinner, the entire course was ordered for a fall-in by the duty officer. It was suspected that some of the boys had gone on FL (French leave) to town and this was a surprise check. The fall-in was delayed and the duty officer was angry. He had all of us on our haunches and soon a full-scale post-dinner PT class commenced.

Before long, the nice clean trousers and white shirts were crumpled, muddy and wet with sweat. Some boys could not hold their meals down after the intense physical activity and messed things up further. The punishment continued unabated through the night...or so it seemed. By the time it was over, some of the weak ones could hardly walk back to their rooms. I for one flopped into my bed without even bothering to remove my shoes or change. Come Sunday morning, some of the cadets (including MP and I!) couldn't eat with their own hands. Our forearms were swollen—much like Popeye from the comic strip—due to the push-ups we had been made to do.

MP and we were soon in the thick of training, though punishments and extra PT and parade continued to fill up our 'spare' time! Those from the Sainik and Military Schools took the rigours better, but the others also managed to settle down in time.

Friendships now began to blossom. First there were the associations formed along common school affiliations, language, place etc. MP had a total of nine friends from school in his batch and they formed his closest friend circle. Thereafter began the bonding with boys from different parts of the country, based on ideas, behaviour and intellect. The true mixing of cultures in the cauldron of the NDA had now begun, and there was no looking back. These bonds were for life—through thick and thin, through combat conditions and social interactions.

BOXING IS introduced at the academy right from the first term. With competitions round the corner, the 'real' boxers are segregated and toughened up. Most of them are from Military or Sainik Schools and have boxed earlier. But all cadets have to perforce fight bouts to get a 'feel' of boxing.

MP describes them, 'The boxing bouts amongst the novices

were not exactly boxing contests as we know them'. Captain Lewin from the Indian Navy, and Commander of the NDA Wing, laid down the rules. 'Just one round', he would say. But the round would continue till he thought it was enough. No scoring, no points, just hit each other till exhaustion. MP adds, 'Captain Lewin would ensconce himself in the centre of the large sofa, leg on leg, pipe rakishly balanced on his lips. The bearded man meant business and his eyes glowered. The sense of intimidation travelled into the boxing ring'. The boxers would keep looking at him through the corner of their eyes for his signal to stop. 'Next!' he would growl. Noses and lips bloodied, the 'boxers' would leave the ring to lick their wounds. Boxing was the first of the lessons taught at NDA to instill the killer instinct.

The boxing ustaad thought MP had natural talent and took him on for special training. He was soon in the squadron boxing team. The boys had to maintain their weight to fight in the correct weight category. But there was a way to beat the system. The cadets would lose three to four kg of weight by undergoing what was called 'blanket treatment' just before it was time to get on the scales. The whole lot of boys would lie down on blankets after a hectic round of physicals and would then be covered with more layers of blankets. Squadron juniors were then made to walk and jump over these bodies, which led to excessive sweating and subsequent loss of weight. The cadet would invariably fight in a lower weight category than his actual weight.

Then the boys would be fed bananas and fluids, which took them back to their original weight! Since all the cadets did this, the whole exercise was an act in futility. The boys realised this but it was a tradition and no one questioned its logic.

The juniors found the activity quite enjoyable since they could 'beat' up their seniors!

The bouts were serious stuff, with medals and glory up for grabs. MP boxed his way into the quarter-finals, defeating three of his course-mates. He was pitted against a 'pro' boxer 'Wangdi' from Bhutan for the bronze. The Bhutanese managed to get a punch into the base of MP's right thumb and broke it early in the bout. Knocked out, MP was taken to the military hospital and sentenced to four weeks in plaster.

MP writes, 'While returning from hospital I mulled over my fate: on the one hand, a win over Wangdi might have culminated in a glittering medal around my neck; on the other hand, the POP cast had rescued my already battered body from further punishment. Who wants to court glory after subjecting your body to extensive beating? I gladly embraced the latter fate'.

With exams around the corner, MP wondered how he was going to write with his fractured right hand. He quickly learnt the art of writing with his left hand and with some practice, he was able to take his tests. Much later, he was to learn to write with his mouth when he didn't have the use of any limbs.

In the second term, it was mandatory to undergo 'novices boxing', whether you were an established boxer or not. Just one bout of three minutes, under the watchful eyes of the divisional officer. Luckily there was no Captain Lewin here and this appeared to be a piece of cake.

'I was pitted against my classmate from school Pramod Kumar', writes MP. 'Punching each other was unthinkable and we planned a feint job; throwing punches spiritedly but not connecting at all.' 'Stop!' said Captain Mehta, the referee.

Asking them their names he snorted, 'Pramod Kumar and Anil Kumar! Brothers?' 'No sir!' both replied in unison. 'Cousins?' No sir again. 'School types then?' he hollered. 'Yes sir', said both, looking at the floor as if they had been caught red-handed.

Smiling, he commanded, 'Boxers, boxxxxx on!' As the sham boxing continued, his temper got the better of him since the deputy commandant was also watching. 'Start bloody boxing', he hissed at them between his teeth. Pramod was a State-level pugilist and MP did not want to be clobbered in any serious fight. MP continues, 'The self-preservation urge smartened me up and I winked at Pramod to throw me a punch. His jab found my face, and luckily, the loud smack was good enough to impress the referee. I grabbed the opportunity, pretended to lose my balance and feigned "knocked out"'.

After the referee failed to get MP back on his feet, Pramod was declared the winner and MP stretchered off the ring. As he went out towards the parked ambulance, he got up and assured the paramedics that he was okay, just a bit stunned. He was let off by the kind doctor on duty and was soon on his way back to the squadron on his cycle, admiring his own theatrics. En route, he was accosted by a fifth-termer who had watched the entire incident. 'Taambi' (all boys from the south were called that), he growled, 'meet me in the squadron', and peddled away.

'Chau' Chaudhary was a 24 carat Jat from Haryana who was the undisputed boxing champion of the academy. Back in the squadron, he made MP don his boxing gloves and punched him as if he was practicing on a punching bag. In MP's words, 'Somehow the bit of boxing I had learnt from Unni Sir at school came in handy. I was able to ward off the ferocious punches to a large extent'.

Much like Captain Lewin, Choudhary ensured that MP got his share of boxing and let him off with a warning. 'Phew! Dog tired, I went to sleep, hitting the bed, thanking Unni Sir profusely for his valuable boxing lessons', MP concludes.

The other troop games for the term were also well-contested. With so many boys wanting to play, the squadron was divided into six strings of players. The first string obviously played with the first string of the opposing squadron. MP played for the top strings in all the games played in the first term and proved his prowess at sport.

AS FAR as academics went, the cadets were split into science and arts stream right at the beginning of term after an aptitude test. They were further distributed into classes from A to F depending on their performance in this exam. The arts classes were numbered 1 to 6. MP was in class A of the science stream. The subjects were easy since it was a repeat of the class 11 and 12 syllabus and all one had to do was listen carefully and be attentive to do well in studies. This was difficult for most due to the heavy dose of outdoor activity and the teachers had a big problem keeping these boys awake and interested.

Drill was an outdoor activity that was new to the cadets. While the boys who came from Sainik School or Military School were already exposed to some form of drill, the drill at NDA was different and more exacting. Hours were spent learning to swing the arms in the correct manner. Standing upright, standing to attention, saluting, marching and turning were all taught to the cadets as if they were toddlers learning to walk.

Halfway through the term, all cadets were required to pass

the Drill Square Test (DST). All those who passed wore the red lanyard on their shoulders and this was a proud moment for each of the boys. Those who didn't have a lanyard were frowned upon. It was a difficult test supervised by none other than the adjutant, a stickler for perfection.

In preparation for the test, khaki uniforms were starched to stiffness, new buttons sewed on, the brass polished and re-polished and the shoes shone until they were black mirrors. The adjutant would inspect each cadet from head to toe as he stood at attention. If you batted even an eyelid, you would be out of the parade square, doing drill with the others who were not yet fit to attempt the test.

Putting his fingers through the belt to check if it was tight enough, the adjutant shouted, 'One more Anil Kumar can pass through this gap! Too loose! Fall out! Failed!' MP was asked to join us 'normal' cadets doing parade in another corner of the ground. He had been chosen by his drill instructor to appear in the first attempt since he was the best of the lot and this failure of his chosen candidate didn't make the instructor happy at all. The drill instructor ordered the boy to run in his shining boots all over the parade ground. The sweat melted the starch in the cotton shorts and shirt and turned them into a gooey mess. Dejected, MP had to wait for the next round of tests. This time he made sure that the belt was so tight that he could hardly breathe when he went to the parade ground. And the adjutant didn't even check his belt this time! 'PASS...NEXT!' and MP was amongst the first few in the course to pass this gruelling test. He wore the lanyard proudly on his left shoulder.

Another benefit of clearing the drill test was 'Liberty' on

Sundays and holidays. Ninety rupees was the pocket money allowance for the month, which could be spent better in town, seeing a movie, eating food of your choice like dosa and idli followed by some ice cream. Once you were out in civvy street, you could ogle at girls too. MP did just that the first weekend that followed, along with some guys who had also passed the test.

Some of us graduated to the second term without passing the drill test. Here there was a sword hanging above the cadet's head. If they failed to make the grade by the middle of the second term, they would be relegated and have to repeat the term. The squadron seniors and drill ustaads put in extra effort to ensure that the test was passed by all. These poor chaps had to change into drill attire after dinner and practise in the squadron parade ground every night. It was a funny sight—cadets in white PT dress with drill boots, anklets and belts!

As at school, MP continued to do well in academics while at the NDA Wing. At the end of the term he passed out amongst the top of the course overall. It was no mean achievement because he was competing with the best of the best. He won a bronze torch for excellence in academics—an honour that he carried through in all his six terms at the academy.

Individual and team medals were also up for grabs in the cross-country race. Practice for the same began in earnest a month before the event, with a large number of endurance-building runs. While some of the guys were naturals at this, for most of us this exercise was the most demanding of the lot—testing our mental and physical stamina to the limit. The only interesting part was running through the open fields behind the Rajneesh Ashram where we could eye some pretty foreigners!

Five months passed in a jiffy. The boys were on their way to becoming men. They had been smoothly and steadily integrated into the fabric of the NDA. Bonds had been formed amongst the course-mates and these would only get stronger as the terms went by. They were getting more open to different foods, different people, and different environments. Leaders were in the making. Barring a few stragglers who stayed on to repeat the first term, most of the cadets were promoted to the second term in June of 1981.

Khadakwasla campus

FIRST WEEK of July, 1981. The second-termers arrived a couple of days before the other cadets and were expected to be settled in by the time the rest of the 1,500 cadets arrived.

They came in hordes in buses with their large black trunks of similar size, standing in front of the huge Cadets Mess, soaking in the atmosphere. The reception centre was set up at the entrance to the mess and there was hustle and bustle as squadrons were allotted, photographs taken and more forms filled.

The NDA campus was huge and awe-inspiring. We were proud to be in one of the finest campuses in the world. As he got off the bus, MP compared the grandeur of the academy with that of his school. The school seemed so small and ordinary now!

A few seniors from each squadron directed the newcomers to their quarters. MP and three of his classmates—G Prakash,

Thomas Kutty Joseph and BS Krishna Kumar—found themselves together in the 'I' or India Squadron located close to the mess. The freshers soon found themselves surrounded by seniors out for some fun.

The juniors were bombarded with a million questions which included some on the academy. 'What is the length of Sudan Block, what is the height of the Ashoka pillar? How many basketball fields are there in the academy?'

'Don't know this much? You're no good!' A little banter and a few laughs later, MP and the others found themselves in their rooms. In a few weeks, all of us were well-versed in the details of the academy; our survival depended on it!

We had to settle down straightaway since the training was to commence on the coming Monday. It was time to go to the local 'Gol' (circular shaped) market to buy supplies and take the long walk to the Mechanical Transport Section where hundreds of maroon bicycles lay parked against one another, ready for issue to the cadets. The squadron colour adorned the front and rear of the cycle, a number painted on each for easy identification. I was issued a brand new bike and was happy about it. But not for long! It became the most coveted machine, and every senior in the squadron wanted to ride it, handing me his battered bicycle instead!

No cadet was allowed to walk around alone at the academy; one had to have a 'squad' consisting of at least four guys to move from place to place. The bikes too couldn't be ridden alone—a squad had to be formed and cycles were seen moving around in fours and sixes. In case one didn't find a squad, the rule was to run along with the cycle from one place to another.

As one went riding around and came across an instructor, the bikers were supposed to stop pedaling, pull their arms straight and the rear guy would shout, 'Savdhaan Chal!' It was quite a comical thing to do but we got used to it soon enough. The ladies we encountered on the way, of course, got the loudest compliments!

Kit laid out, items in the trunk put away in the cupboard, the trunk itself snugly fitted under the bed, the bed set in the style that is only taught at the academy (and at hospitals!) and the room cleaned of the cobwebs of the last term, the boys were ready to begin training. The course was now divided into 12 squadrons, and therefore one found about 20 to 25 cadets of a course in each squadron, consisting of approximately 120 boys.

A bit of ragging was customary at the academy in our times. Although cases of man-handling were few and far between, the normal 'punishments' in terms of rolling (front-rolling, back-rolling and side-rolling), running, standing upside down and the like were acceptable to all. In MP's words, 'As cadets, one couldn't deduce the raison d'être for the punishments meted out to us as much of it was expiatory, not deterrent by nature; just like the hills hemming the campus, punishments too were woven into the warp and weft of our life'.

The second-termers were dismissed as the lowest form of life and were at the receiving end almost all the time. The sixth-termers were too high up in the foodchain to even notice them. But the third- to fifth-termers hounded the freshers.

After the first few outdoor periods, one was expected to have a quick shower, change into uniform, go for breakfast, come back, collect one's cycle, form a squad and proceed to the classes. All this was to be achieved in 55 minutes flat. The second-termers had to come to their rooms, change into night dress, put on their dressing gowns and go to the bathroom. Here they were expected to wait for the seniors to move out before they got a chance to get under the showers. After the bath, one was expected to get back into night dress and gown and rush back to the cabin to get ready. These second-termers or dukkis as they were called, were forced to follow every procedure to the T; as one went up the ladder, little by little, concessions were allowed. The sixth-termer was at liberty to walk to the bathroom in his shorts or with a towel around his waist, sans gown etc! So, with most of the time spent in getting ready following protocols, there was little time for breakfast for the poor second termers. Once in a while we did manage to wrap some toast in paper napkins and carried it to our classes.

One second-termer was tasked to distribute biscuits to all the sixth-termers early every morning. He used his satchel (used to carry books to class) to carry these and put them above the doorframe. Every sixth-termer generally 'adopted' a dukki to look after his needs and called him an 'undie'—short for understudy! They ran some minor errands like getting tea and sometimes running to the market to get some essentials or snacks or to get notes from friends in other squadrons. There was a sixth-termer who asked his undie to do his homework too!

Second-termers didn't mind, since no one could touch them when they were on an errand for the sixth-termer. The biscuit man could save a lot of biscuits and keep them safe in his trunk to be consumed in the dark of the night or traded for some favour from his course-mates! This was an opportunity to break protocol and get their own tea along with their senior's mug while all the third-, fourth- and fifth-termers waited in line. Sometimes, a large-hearted sixth-termer would call his undie and give him an extra bite of the snacks to commend the good job he was doing.

At the mess, the seniors sat around these rookies and taught them table manners—often the hard way! The seniors often quizzed the youngsters on their knowledge of the academy during meals. While they bombarded you with questions, they gorged on the food while we had to keep our hands under the table looking longingly at the food in our plates. If a senior asked you a question you couldn't answer, the meal would turn into a nightmare! You could end up eating 'square meals'—the spoon going in a square pattern from plate to mouth. Before every spoonful one had to ask permission: Please excuse me sir, please may I have my next spoonful?

Some seniors would ask them to put salt in their porridge or just order them to close their plates and 'carry on'...but in hindsight, MP thought, all these exercises made the cadet extremely tough.

A compendium of the punishments doled out to the cadets would be a lengthy one. A fifth-termer once asked a group of cadets, including MP, 'What is the length of the squadron corridor?' They were all geared up to go for a Sunday movie at the auditorium and had formed a squad to leave. Eighty metres, someone guessed. 'Wipe that smile off your face', the senior growled. 'Nothing is bloody measured in metres at the academy.' Summoning a third-termer passing by, he barked, 'Sort these guys out!' and walked away. Soon the boys were measuring the length in units of front-rolls, side-rolls, frog jumps, crocodile jumps and so on! Sweaty and dusty, they still made it to the movie.

'Puttee parade' involved darting to one's cabin, changing into the ordered uniform and reporting back within a stipulated time. From mess dress to full-scale military order to riding rig, all accomplished one after the other. At the end of such a punishment, the cabin would be in absolute disarray and the senior would then order a cabin cupboard inspection, meaning getting things back in order.

The opposite of the cabin cupboard inspection was the 'heckle order', which simply meant that all the items in the room were to be packed into the trunks and locked as if one were going home for the term break! This was again followed by a kit muster (a check of all items on inventory issued to the cadet) and a cabin cupboard. Some Sundays were utilised by the duty officer to 'sort out' some of the senior courses too. The second-termers were now called in to help the seniors get their rigs ready as they rushed about the corridors of the squadron. MP writes, 'A dose of kit muster and cabin cupboard can make even a hardy ascetic lose his marbles!' Often, we youngsters were asked to procure kit items from other squadrons to make up the deficiencies when such an exercise was undertaken. In any case, we were taught to 'manage' anything and everything about our lives at the NDA—one had to learn to share and care.

Looking at any senior undergoing any form of punishment was taboo. The juniors were forbidden to come out of the rooms whenever such a punishment was in progress, and just in case you ran into such a situation, you were expected to 'look down' or turn the other way. Even during the regular fall-ins at the squadron, if the Cadet Sergeant Major (CSM) decided to bark at some senior-termer, his juniors would put their heads down, as if in apology for his misdemeanours. If one met a senior in the squadron going to or returning from his punishment run, the juniors were supposed to look the other way or simply turn around and run away! Strange were some of the traditions at the NDA! But looking back, I really do believe that all this was required to turn us into good, rugged military men.

Second-termers were not supposed to walk. They had to run, no matter where they were. You could be going to the washroom, but you had to run! In some squadrons, the second-termers were 'excused' from using the staircase. They had to shimmy up the rope or come sliding down to the required floor (NDA squadrons had two floors). It was meant to 'toughen up' the boys. Boys who did well in outdoor activities were exempt from such discomfiture. If you proved yourself worthy at any activity, be it games or studies, you could walk, not run, eat without being bothered in the mess and be saved some 'unofficial' punishments.

Halfway through the second term, the cadets were deeply ensconced in the matrix of the academy and things slowly eased.

'Seventh heaven' was MP's favourite punishment. Every room had a grill mesh fitted above the door all along the length of the room. Seventh heaven simply meant that one had to leap up to clutch the seventh horizontal rung of the lattice from the top and then recite the NDA prayer while dangling there. Once, MP hit upon a novel idea to get back at a painful senior. During his afternoon siesta on a Sunday, MP went close to the senior's room and jumped on to seventh heaven, howling out the NDA prayer: 'Oh God, help us to keep ourselves physically strong, mentally awake and morally straight...' The prayer was halted midway by the irate senior, who rushed out to terminate the punishment session in progress. But it was only MP, and no senior to supervise the punishment. MP bluffed that a senior had asked him to do this earlier in the day. 'You see', MP said, 'the NDA groundwork is meant to not only toughen one physically and mentally, but also to make the cadet streetsmart and a survivor.'

ACADEMIC INSTRUCTORS at NDA fell into three categories. First, the permanent staff of academicians, selected through the Union Public Service Commission (UPSC), each with long experience of teaching and handling cadets. Second, the temporary teachers who stood in to fill vacancies not filled by the UPSC. They were relatively young and did not have much 'military' experience. And third, instructors from the education branch of the three services, there on a three-year tenure.

The permanent staff was the strictest. Some of them had the habit of reporting cadet behaviour to the divisional officer directly rather than choosing punitive action themselves. This was bad since it meant missing out on breakfast when called to meet the divisional officers, who would slap on 'restrictions' or EDs (extra drills) without batting an eyelid. The boys generally behaved themselves in their classes since the cost of misbehaving with such instructors was high.

Sitting with MP one day and reminiscing about the mischief we'd get up to at the academy, he reminded me of an incident I had long forgotten. There was a very strict lady teacher who had a habit of throwing the duster or a piece of chalk at cadets she found sleeping in class. One of MP's classmates was dropping off to sleep when he saw a missile flying towards him through his droopy eyes. His reactions were good and he managed to catch the flying duster with his hand, and went and handed it back to the teacher with an innocent smile, with the class in splits of laughter. The class continued without further mishap.

Reaching the squadron after classes, the student was summoned to the Squadron Commander's office. 'What did you do today?' barked the officer. 'Nothing.' 'Then why is there a charge-sheet against you from your geography instructor?' The bewildered boy explained what had happened.

A cynical smile appeared on the commander's face as he read out the charge: 'Giving meaningful looks to a lady instructor!' 'Sir, there are so many pretty instructors around, why would I give meaningful looks to her?' the boy blurted out. The commander chuckled, and read out the punishment. 'Three restrictions for giving meaningful looks to an instructor. Four more for bad choice!' MP and I had a hearty laugh.

During another visit to the paraplegic home, MP reminisced about the most important piece of equipment at the NDA—the 'safety pin'! It held literally everything together, and was always to be carried clipped to the strap of the satchel. I remember MP telling me about his squadron mate who had all the different buttons sewed on to small square pieces of cloth of the various uniforms we were issued. All through his six terms he never sewed a button on to any of his uniforms. He just used the safety pin to attach it to the uniform in question! Till finally one day he was caught and punished. The punishment—to sew a hundred buttons on to a handkerchief! Besides holding our uniforms together, the safety pin was used for a myriad other things—from deflating tyres of 'enemy' cycles to picking teeth! 'The NDA was held together by the ubiquitous safety pin!' laughed MP.

The best instructors for us cadets were undoubtedly the temporary staff. They were young and naive and we could easily take them for a ride. Secondly, one could sleep peacefully in their classes without fear of retribution, and lastly, they would give out the 'important' questions before the exams so that we could do well in their subjects!

Sir Barnes Neville Wallis, the English scientist and inventor of the bouncing bomb of *Dambusters* fame, had philosophised: 'Struggle is the sauce of life. Character is developed by endurance, by constantly facing and beating hardship.' To this, MP adds, 'Given the strenuous nature of the cadet's life, I guess the NDA was inspired by the Wallis doctrine that our talents develop best only when catalysed by pressure and tension!'

Remaining afloat

LEARNING TO swim was an important and inescapable requirement. All cadets were required to swim a minimum of 50 metres of breaststroke to pass out of the academy. Surprisingly, swimming did not come naturally to this boy from the backwaters of Kerala. Immediately on arrival at the academy, MP's swimming training began in earnest. The memory of his struggles in the sea waters at Kovalam a few years ago shadowed him.

Initially, till swimming was mastered, the cadets were taken to the Olympic-sized pool on almost all days of the week; especially the ones who were known as 'sinkers' or non-swimmers. The others, who could pass muster, could go and play games, do PT etc. The sinkers would be thrown en masse into the pool with red caps, the instructors following in white caps for easy identification. While some managed to splash around and hang on to the sides, the panic-stricken sinkers took the instructors down, holding on to them for dear life. MP was determined to give it his best shot. The PT ustaad promised MP that if he got through the minimum qualifying requirement, he would take him for training in gymnastics—a sport MP loved. Very soon he managed to pass the swimming test and was spared the agony of long hours in the water.

But swimming by itself was not enough. Each cadet had to carry out an intimidating jump from the 7-metre board. It was a test of nerves for most and a Waterloo for some. The instructors and divisional officers were present in abundance when this activity was in progress—to check if the young boys under their charge had the courage to jump. The ustaads were all over the pool too. Plus there was a rescue party with a large bamboo pole with a red flag at its end. The 7-metre jump test was to be passed not once but every term. In the fifth and sixth term, one had to jump from 10 metres! Jumping into water from a good 30-plus feet height sounded absurd to MP. But then he often thought to himself, 'What if there is a still higher jump test to conquer?'

It was a one-way street for the cadets, up the ladder to the diving board. The academy looked like a picture-perfect postcard from up there, the pool a stamp in the corner. 'Look straight ahead and step off the board', ordered the instructor. The boy jumped, sucking in a deep breath, fear churning his stomach, a hundred thoughts going through his mind in the few seconds of flight. As he went under, there'd be a big whoosh, the size of the splash indicating the angle of entry. If one entered at a high angle one could get a red face, back or chest, depending on which part hit the water first. After a bubbly path to almost the bottom of the pool, one surfaced after what seemed like a lifetime under water, gasping, sputtering and coughing, splashing feverishly with arms and legs to stay afloat. The sinkers would invariably be so disoriented and distraught that the long bamboo pole had to be used to fish them out.

Those who completed the jump could watch the rest of the pantomime unfold. Some cadets went up the steps and wanted to come down the same way, trying every trick in the book to convince the ustaad on the diving board to let them descend. Often, they found themselves plummeting into the water, nudged by the instructor. But there were a few tough nuts like G Prakash.

Despite numerous commands given from below by Divisional Officer Flight Lieutenant SC Mishra, GP would not loosen his grip on the railings, his knuckles turning white. A fifth-termer, Cadet Aggarwal, was sent to bolster the effort. A minor scuffle ensued and the boys below waited for the frail GP to come flying down. Nothing of the sort happened. GP's perseverance won out and he managed to edge both his assailants into the pool! MP concludes, 'Aided by some un-understood law of prehensility, our man clung on to the railings, a la Spiderman in his swimming costume, summoned energy from somewhere to do a toilsome pull-up and get back on to the 7-metre board, majestically standing there unvanquished'.

With no one left on top of the board, GP looked down sheepishly at Flight Lieutenant Mishra who promptly ordered him to come down the steps to face his wrath. The audience chuckled. GP finally jumped, though much later, when he was threatened with relegation and loss of seniority.

A cadet who lost a term for any reason was called a 'Brigadier' while one who lost two was referred to as a 'General'. These relegated cadets attended classes and trained with the junior courses but their affiliation with their original course never ceased. So one could be a General in the fourth term and get all the perks and privileges of the sixth term; thus, this man actually enjoyed three sixth terms at the academy! These relegated cadets were a special lot who enjoyed a larger number of senior terms at the academy, and we rookies looked at them in awe. Though we were told that cadets who lost three terms were called Field Marshals, we never encountered any. I suppose there must have been a few people in the history of NDA who completed their three-year training in four-and-a-half years!

Horse sense

HORSE RIDING was another activity that almost all the cadets at the academy were unfamiliar with. The first few days on the saddle caused a few bruises and cuts in unwanted places, but they had to be endured. All the horses were quite well-trained. They understood the commands of the instructor. Tham (halt), Bayen mu'd (left turn), Trot and Gallop were the common commands and before the cadet realised it, the horse had obeyed. It was as if the horse was on auto-pilot. The animals had a sixth sense by which they could discern the confidence level of the rider, and they used this awareness to take the rider for a literal ride!

There were some wayward horses too. Once in a while when they had had enough, they would buck and jump, dislodging the unsuspecting cadet from the saddle. Seizing the opportunity, the horse would run back to the comfort of the stables even before the poor boy reacted to grab the reins. The long walk through the shrub and slush in riding breeches and large boots was by no means comfortable. Many a time early on in his training, a frisky horse left MP high and dry in the middle of the fields and he had to trudge all the way back.

Come fourth term, the cadets had to pass an 'equitation test'; that is, they had to clear the minimum level of handling and riding a horse. The grand finale was a 'lane jumping test' which was quite out of the comic strips. On an order, the gates to an obstacle course would be opened, and the horse galloped and jumped from one obstacle to the other with the boy clutching on to his mane or saddle for dear life. To top it all, one was supposed to sing out one's roll number, name and squadron as the animal went through his routine. MP thought it a wonder that he was still atop the animal at the end of this duel, thus passing with minimum qualifying mark in equitation.

'Hurting from the saddle-bite I picked up during my maiden riding, I could not but wonder why future military officers should undergo horse-riding. Only later it dawned on me that riding made horse sense', writes MP. 'Having put up with a generation of cadets, the NDA horses knew who was adept and expressed their exasperation at lousy horsemanship by shaking their muzzles in disbelief, neighing, bucking and kicking. The rider had to earn the respect of the animal, period. Analogically, an officer had to earn the respect of his subordinates to become an effective leader.'

SUNDAY WAS the day off for the cadets. The weekend actually began with no official activity after the lunch break on Saturday. An English movie was screened on Saturdays and a Hindi one on

Sunday. Some beautiful classics and war movies were screened and attendance for some of the good war movies was compulsory. The Hindi movies were the typical song and dance romances which provided wholesome entertainment.

The massive Habibullah Auditorium that screened the movies and all other motivational talks and debates was able to seat close to 2,000. It was constructed in three tiers and had the best of seating and acoustics. While the lower floor was reserved for the NDA instructors and families along with the sixth-termers, the rest of the academy sat as per seniority, with the youngest occupying the top floor.

I remember one movie with some scintillating songs where the actress gyrated rather provocatively. Some of the boys sighed loudly and lustfully. A shock wave went through the auditorium! The academy cadet adjutant was asked to investigate who was responsible for this ungentlemanly conduct. But it was impossible to find out.

That night after the movie, we were first given a lecture on officer-like behaviour and then told to fall-in outside the auditorium. The saabs were called in and the collective punishment began. What a sight it was! Almost 1,500 of us running, jumping, rolling, haunching and what have you.

After Sunday breakfast, it was time to venture into the colours and sights of the bustling city of Pune on 'liberty'. But all those who had been awarded official punishments had to complete them on Sundays and holidays. It involved getting ready in dungarees, wearing full-scale military packs and running 8-odd km around the academy. In addition to the physical part of the punishment, the cadet was kept busy reporting to the duty officer at specific timings in different uniforms through the day and night. The lazy ones or those who did not have adequate money for the outing stayed back at the academy and lazed through the day, catching up on sleep.

The only girls one saw were at the local market which was frequented only on weekends. The bakery and sweetmeat shops also had some pretty girls behind the counters to boost footfalls from the cadets. In our time, one of the officers posted as the equitation officer had a very pretty wife who had acted in some Bollywood films and spent a lot of time riding. She was a major reason why cadets opted for 'hack-rides' or cross-country riding on Sundays!

The bulk of the time on liberty was spent ogling at pretty girls who were found in abundance at select places in Pune like the Deccan Gymkhana and the Pune Camp area. In those times, very few of us cadets had steady girl-friends to strut around with and the few who did were asked to request their girl-friends to bring other girls along for the evening. Interacting with the opposite sex and sitting through a meal and a movie was a welcome change.

During study periods in the evenings the windows were left open and cadets facing the main road had a view of the traffic. Whenever a pretty lass was spotted, one of the second-termers was ordered to go and make a loud announcement from the central lobby in the squadron. Books were set aside as everyone rushed to the windows to have a good look. This harmless mischief in a male-dominated environment allowed some respite to the young minds.

The academic block also had a few young lady instructors. They received the smartest salutes, boys were least likely to sleep in their classes and were actually able to improve their grades as a consequence! Then there were pretty daughters of instructors to be admired, especially at the movie hall, at formal tea parties or dinners and at the market. A few of us actually got hooked for life at the academy itself, falling in love with the instructors' daughters and getting married later.

Passing out parade

THE TERMS wore on. Besides doing well in academics, MP was doing fairly well in the outdoors too, physical training remaining his forte. The PT instructor thought that MP had the ideal flexibility and upper body strength to take up gymnastics. The required PT tests were no big deal for the strapping young man and he managed to complete his higher-level tests too. This gave him ample time to practise display-level gymnastics, including the horse, beam and mat-work. So lithe was his body that he learnt to do the back flip and forward somersault without any effort. Sometimes seniors in the academic block asked him to do a back flip in slow motion—in uniform—and MP did it with flourish. When caught with a group for combined punishment, the sergeant on duty would ask him to demonstrate his handspring or back flip on the roadside.

During the end of term, with the exams behind them, the academy was abuzz with activity to showcase all aspects of training. Parents and relatives of the passing out course were invited to witness all that the NDA cadet could do. Proud parents came to see their wards and friends doing mass PT, drill, horse riding displays and gymnastics. It was also time for the academy to rehearse for the majestic passing out parade (POP). A majority of the boys took part in the parade and the only ones excused were the cadets taking part in the displays and the entertainment programmes which constituted the 'end of term activities'.

MP was chosen to be part of the gymnastics team from the third term itself, and continued in it right up to the end of his tenure at the NDA. In fact, during his passing out parade, MP was invited to do some of his stunts in a special display. At that stage, the quality of his flips and rolls could put some of the PT ustaads to shame.

At drill too MP did well. He was good at marching and was chosen to be part of the 'cane orderly' contingent in his fourth term. The cane orderlies were supposed to be the best at drill. The sound of their boots would be music to the ears and a motivation to the guys standing on parade. It was a treat to watch their synchronised drill as they came down the steps escorting the chief guest. It required a colossal amount of sweat and practice, but it made you the hero of the academy. Unfortunately, MP did not make it to the final selection. He was disappointed, but took it in his stride.

An important aspect of training at the NDA are the camps that are planned in the second (Camp Green Horn), fourth (Camp Rover) and sixth (Camp Torna) terms. The second term camp is just an introduction to basic battle concepts like map-reading, navigation, compass-reading and other simple activities, besides some endurance training. The fourth term camp is considered one of the toughest camps for cadets of that age anywhere in the world. The sixth term camp is conducted to introduce the cadets to simulated battle conditions and also involves visits to various defence establishments. This camp is held at the culmination of all training at the NDA. Now the sixth-termers get ready to pass out. All these camps are designed to instill and reinforce the 'never say die' attitude in the cadets.

Queen Elizabeth paid the academy a visit during our sixth term, in 1983. The entire academy was bedecked in her honour, the cadets excited to see such famous royalty. MP was a Divisional Cadet Captain (DCC) and leading a part of the contingent of the parade that was presented to the queen. So impressed was she with the standard of the parade that in her speech she exclaimed, 'I have never seen such a large parade being commanded with such precision just by vocal word of command. I would like to import this technology to England'.

A six-course lunch was planned in her honour which every cadet from those days remembers. We had a practice lunch which a minister from Delhi was supposed to attend. He was delayed for some reason and 1,600 hungry men had to wait behind their chairs watching their soup go cold. To top it all, the minister seemed to be in a hurry to get back and he whizzed through the six courses in quick-time. I don't think he had been briefed that the entire academy would have to synchronise the closing of their plates for each course with him. The end result was that we were left hungry and a large amount of food was not consumed.

Luckily for us, after the VIP left, we were allowed to sit down at our tables again and eat. The Queen, on the other hand, was very considerate. She knew that we cadets would require more time to eat and so she took each course very slow. We were a happy lot and enjoyed the special meal thoroughly.

THE DCC at the NDA controls 30 to 35 cadets in his 'division'. He wears a grey epaulette on his shoulders and carries a cane as he marches around the academy. The four DCCs of the squadron report to the Squadron Cadet Captain (SCC). The Cadet Sergeant Major (CSM) is the dynamo of the squadron who is actually responsible for running the show. He gets the squadron fighting fit for the various competitions; the squadron's performance often hinges on how this man manages to plan, coordinate and motivate the boys to perform. This finally translates to where the squadron stands in the overall ranking.

How MP became a DCC is an interesting story. It was nearing the end of the fifth term. As the sixth-termers go away on their final camp before the passing out, the reins of the academy pass on to the fifth-termer 'understudy' appointments who take over command and control until the end of the term and thereafter in their sixth term too. MP was nominated Battalion Cadet Adjutant (BCA), quite a prestigious appointment at the academy. He was to be an 'academy appointment', a rung higher than the 'squadron appointment'. As the understudy, he took over the job as soon as the 64th course went for their camp.

It is a tradition for the squadron commander to invite the graduating course to a tea party in the last week before the passing out parade. Along with them, he also invites the future cadet appointments or understudies as they are called. In addition to this social event there are a number of school and squadron social evenings planned where the sixth-termers are bid farewell. It so happened that the squadron commander's tea and MP's school social function were planned on the same day.

MP was in a dilemma where to head. He went and saw the notice board to check if his name featured in the list of invitees to the squadron commander's tea. He breathed a sigh of relief when he saw that only the future squadron appointments figured in the list. He now thought that he was free to attend the school social, which for the cadets, was one of the most important events at the end of term. It was time to say goodbye to schoolmates.

'As I was about to leave the squadron for the social that evening, Vasudesh Arya, a second-termer, rushed to me and conveyed the message that I was to head for the squadron commander's tea', MP writes. He had to make a quick decision. The excitement of attending the school social got the better of him. He thought to himself and decided not to change his plan. Looking into the boy's eyes, he remarked, 'You haven't seen me!...Understood?'

'Yes sir!' answered the confused boy and sprinted away.

After enjoying a pleasant evening with his old school pals, eating good food and reminiscing about old times, MP returned to his squadron. Entering the central lobby, he saw that the squadron office lights were on and the four divisional officers of his squadron were pacing the corridor. Confronting MP as soon as he stepped in, they asked curtly, 'Why were you missing from the squadron commander's tea?'

MP used all his theatrical skills to convince the four that he was not part of the list and feigned a stunned look. 'Didn't *anybody* tell you that you had to attend?' they asked. 'NO SIR!' MP replied confidently, holding to his part of the story. 'ARYA! Come here!' someone shouted. The frightened second-termer appeared as if from thin air and standing next to MP testified like a well-rehearsed parrot.

The divisional officer, Captain Kataria, smirked and looked questioningly at MP. 'So? WHY DID YOU SKIP?' he bellowed.

MP blurted out truthfully without looking up, 'My school social was more important than the squadron commander's tea'. 'As far as the NDA was concerned, there could not be a more temerarious and impudent answer', MP wrote. 'I had committed the grave error of demeaning an officer for which I deserved the guillotine.' He really had managed to get on the wrong side of the establishment. While they exhausted themselves with some choice expletives, MP could only look down and endure the humiliation.

A decision was taken on the spot. MP was to be stripped of the battalion cadet adjutant rank. Since he was high enough in overall merit, MP had to be given some appointment and therefore became a DCC in his sixth term. The DivOs kept him on a tight leash through his sixth term. They had been genuinely hurt by MP's behaviour.

Sitting at his computer as a quadriplegic many years later, MP concluded, 'Yet I passed out from NDA fourth in the order of merit. The first three are honoured with the President's Gold, Silver and Bronze medals during the passing out parade. For someone leading the dependent life of a quadriplegic for the past 18 years, regurgitating the nuggets of past glory provides me fleeting cheer and a break from the humdrum. Though I nurse no regret about this incident, it still hurts. Winning a medal, even gold, was there for the asking, but it's not there on the mantelpiece. That's one achievement less to reminisce about, a few moments less to swell my paralysed chest with pride'.

Learning to fly

INTO THEIR sixth term now, the cadets were introduced to flying for the first time. Most of the boys were raw and the only time they had experienced the joy of being in the air was maybe on a giant-wheel. MP now realised how gruelling the requirements for the air force are.

To be a good pilot, you needed to be good at various aviation-related subjects too.

It was time to get serious about studying again. The first five terms had been a piece of cake. Now it was time to sift the chaff from the grain. MP quickly got down to mastering the basics. The instructors often felt that he asked too many questions, as if he was trying to show off how much he knew. But I think his intention was just to get his basics strong. This would serve him well as he graduated to much more complex flying regimens once he joined the air force.

The flying training at NDA was carried out at the Glider Drome, a huge flat piece of land nestled between two hills at the eastern edge of the campus. A rudimentary airstrip existed here that at best could allow a small airplane to land. The NDA, in those times, had primitive gliders like the Sedberg of 1957 vintage, the Eon Olympia of 1960 and the India-made Rohini of 1968 vintage on which the cadets were given the first feel of flying.

To get airborne, a steel cable was attached to the front end of the glider. At the other end, about 500-odd metres away, was a pulley run by a rickety old petrol engine which pulled in this cable and provided the much-needed forward speed for the aeroplane to get off the ground. Red and white flags were used to signal the pulley operator to commence pulling once the aeroplane was ready for takeoff. Two cadets ran alongside for the initial phase of the takeoff so that the wing tips didn't graze the ground.

As the glider went up, at about 1,000 feet above ground, the cable was released and the cadet got about four minutes of air experience in one 'launch'. If there were thermals or a nice strong breeze, it would be a little more. MP sat waiting his turn to get up in the air. As one of the gliders took off, one could clearly hear the instructor's voice from 1,000 feet above along with the whoosh of the glider wings through the air.

When the course reached sixth term for flying, just two of these machines were available on flight line. One day as one of the launches was in progress, one of the cadets running alongside the wing tripped and fell right into the wing. The red flag was immediately raised and the takeoff abandoned. While the cadet in question got a mouthful from the instructor, everyone gathered around the aeroplane to see the extent of the damage. A biggish rupture was seen in the fabric of the wing. The plane was grounded and taken in for repairs. Due to non-availability of the special bonding glue and the wet weather, this aeroplane was not available for most of the term and flying training had to be truncated with only one glider available.

So only four launches per cadet were possible—16 minutes of air experience was far too little for the boys to graduate to the jets that were to be flown at the Air Force Academy (AFA). But nothing could be done about that. Except to label it the 'Bicycles to Jets' course!

MP did very well in the 'service subjects', that is, subjects related to the air force and flying. He was awarded the 'Wings' towards the end of the course and these were proudly worn on all uniforms. This was a smaller and maroon-coloured version of the actual white embroidered 'Flying Wing' that the cadets were aspiring to earn the next year at the AFA.

The passing out parade of the 65th Course was planned on December 10, 1983. Preparations began weeks before. All academic exams were over and done with and the books returned. Cycles and the other kit were to be returned a few days before departure. In fact, the blue patrol uniform, shoes and other items of uniform used for the passing out were to be returned immediately after the parade and prior to the departure for home.

Celebration was in the air. Three years had passed like a dream, a dream no one would like to forget for the rest of their lives. What now remained was the convocation ceremony and the last official dinner—the Academy Dinner Night. Parents were to arrive a day prior to the parade and be accommodated in one of the squadron buildings, especially vacated for this.

During the parade, the passing out course forms up in the centre of the parade ground and marches past the dais out of the parade ground, saluting the reviewing officer and the flag-mast. Six fighter aircraft from the local base at Lohegaon carry out a low-level flypast over the dais to wish the passing out course God Speed and Good Luck. In formation of two groups of three cadets each around both sides of the mast, the passing out course exits up the steps that lead out of the parade ground and into the Science Block. The rest of the academy exits through the far end of the parade ground into the Quarter Master Fort.

MP had a vivid and rather interesting story to tell about the passing out parade. The reviewing officer was none other than Air Chief Marshal Dilbagh Singh and incidentally, his nephew, Cadet MJS Bains, was also passing out. However, due to some issues related to discipline, Bains could not attend the minimum required parade practices and was disqualified from participating by Adjutant, Major Daniels, a strict disciplinarian and taskmaster.

Bains pleaded with all and sundry but the answer from all quarters was a resounding no. Since it was his uncle who was reviewing the parade, Bains was petrified about the ignominy if his uncle should find out the reason for his absence. He decided to take the law into his own hands. On the day of the parade, Bains, in all his passing out regalia, went and hid in the hedges bordering the far end of the parade ground. His intention was to join the marching contingent as they turned into review order during the march past.

As the parade progressed, a drill ustaad noticed a rustling in the hedges and went to check. As he confronted Bains, Bains did what he had been taught—he went on the offensive to get out of the tight corner, startling the ustaad. He ran out of the bushes towards the ustaad and suddenly veered away, running into the parade ground, masked by the marching contingents. The drill ustaad was in no mood to give up and followed, shouting, '*Yeh* Cadet! *Tham*! (Stop!)'

Bains was now close to his course-mates' contingent and joined in the front column just as the drill ustaad caught him by his lanyard. The ustaad had to quickly let go of Bains since the contingent was now coming in view of hundreds of spectators. Bains started to march as if he had been in the parade all along, creating a blank file much to the consternation of his course-mates. Due to this, the entire formation of the passing out contingent went for a toss. When MP walked past the dais to the tune of *Auld Lang Syne* during the slow march later, he saw that he had no one to pair with his group on the other side of the rostrum. It had all been due to that one man!

Bains was produced before an extremely angry adjutant at the end of the parade. He was awarded punishments to be completed after the passing out—an event that had not occurred in the history of the academy! Incidentally, Bains was to die in an air-crash about eight months later, and many years later MP wrote the story of the crash in a newspaper.

No one from MP's family attended his passing out. The folks at home were too shy to leave the confines of the village, says Sheeja. Plus Acchan was fully involved in local politics and could not risk being away even for a short duration. There was, however, a parallel celebration in Chirayinkeezhu on that day. Amma made a feast at home and also gave away food to the old and needy while Acchan went around the village distributing sweets to all. It was a happy day in the village 1,578 km away from Pune. They were not even aware that MP had passed out 4th in the merit of the course, missing the President's Medal by his own folly.

Writing many years later, MP summarises the training at NDA thus: 'The camaraderie we fostered at NDA was cast in shared sweat, hunger, torment, fracas, even tomfoolery. Since our ties were born out of enduring hardship together, ours are 24-carat bonds that would easily pass the test of both, time and trials. To me, this steadfast camaraderie is the most perdurable gift NDA gave us, and this togetherness is what makes the alumni an unbeatable force, in both war and peace.'

The NDA motto, 'Service Before Self', embodies the quintessence of this first-rate cradle of military leadership. Whether it was managing kit or inventing alibis, feigning ignorance or making yourself scarce when the going got tough, the academy taught you how to survive and live a full life. 'It taught one the language and grammar of survival', MP summarises.

'When the going gets tough, the tough get going' is a truism that has been heard at NDA over generations. For the military man, this is absolutely true. But what the NDA teaches is to sift through the multitude of tasks, disregard the ones that are redundant and wasteful, and take the ones that require your energies by the horns and to their logical conclusion. A little selective, but important for longevity and survival.

The course report of Cadet Anil Kumar MP at the end of his sixth term reads:

Physical Attributes—PT—Well Above Average, Games—Above Average, Swimming—High Average, Equitation—Average and Drill—High Average.

Final Grading—Academics—First Class, Service Subjects —Above Average and Officer Like Qualities (OLQ)—Above Average

Overall CGPA—6.84, Rank 4/269.

The remarks at the end of the report read, 'He strived hard to achieve the best at the academy and got the best All Round Air Force Cadet. He has held his appointment as the Divisional Cadet Captain with responsibility. He should, however, be more assertive and go into more details. "Above Average" officer material'.

Viva la NDA.

Jet jockey

AT THE end of the rigorous three-year training, MP enjoyed a break at home before he joined the Air Force Academy at Dundigal, near Hyderabad, as a flight cadet. Friends and relatives from the neighbouring villages came over to see the strapping young 'pilot officer' in the making, listening in awe to his stories about his gliding experience at the NDA. He was going to be the first son of the small village to take to the skies.

Activities at the AFA were mostly cerebral. We were there to hone our thinking, reasoning and organising abilities as we prepared to fly. We were much more mature now, out of our teens and some in our early-20s.

With outdoor activity taking a backseat, the aim of the 'pre-flying training' was to see the boys filling up cockpits. The piston engine trainer called the HT-2 had been phased out of service just a course earlier and now we had to start flying the Hindustan Jet Trainer (HJT-16), popularly known as the 'Kiran'. Flying was almost two months away with the interceding months utilised for ground training.

'One more year to go to get the coveted flying badge at the passing out parade', thought MP. Eighty-nine cadets landed up for the 134 Pilots Course at AFA in January 1984. While 51 of us were from NDA, a small number joined as direct entry candidates after doing six months of ab-initio training at Coimbatore, in western Tamil Nadu. These boys had been subjected to training similar to the sixth term at NDA, so they were ready to train alongside us. Some naval cadets, along with two commissioned officers of the Indian Navy, were also part of this course.

All of us went through the ground conversion syllabus on the aircraft in addition to studying a large number of aviation-related subjects. MP loved this part since he was inclined to science; and as a curious boy, his concepts were more or less clear. The subjects ranged from complicated aero engines and aerodynamics to meteorology, airmanship, navigation, aviation medicine and many more—sixteen subjects in all needed to be mastered. The scientific content of all these subjects fascinated MP and he was able to grasp the essentials of aviation very quickly.

The young pilots were familiarised with the system that went into making the aircraft fly. In a few days, we were split into groups of three to four and allotted an instructor; and thus we called each other 'co-pupils'. Learning all the 'checks and procedures' pertaining to the aircraft was an arduous task. We were now issued the first items of special flying clothing which included two pairs of blue overalls, a pair of chamois leather flying gloves, a small first aid kit, helmet with oxygen mask and the most special flying boots which all the other non-flying boys eyed with envy.

Each aircraft has a checklist and every pilot must know these procedures verbatim: how the aircraft is to be checked on ground before flight, pre-flight checks, start-up procedures, checks before takeoff, checks in the air, checks before landing and a hundred more. Each of us 'flyboys' was expected to have the emergency drills and basics of the aircraft at his fingertips, and before venturing anywhere near an aircraft we had to undergo what was called a 'gen test'. Passing marks were 100 per cent for checks and emergency procedures and a little less for technical knowledge. These tests had to be passed in the grades specified before flying could commence.

We were all a bit apprehensive as the days to take to the skies came closer. We knew that just a few of the 89 cadets would get to go 'solo' and through the first phase of flying. The dropout rates at this stage were high, and the instructors often threatened, 'Keep your bags ready; if you do not perform, you will have to go to the army or navy or join the ground duty branches'. 'There are no runners-up here', they always explained. 'A military pilot is a special breed and you have to prove yourself "special"', said his instructor to MP.

There was scarcely time to breathe. We lived and dreamed checks, procedures and emergency actions. Sundays and spare time were utilised for 'room simulator' or 'chair flying' training. In those days there was a rudimentary cockpit simulator available at the AFA to practise the 'cockpit drills'. With so many of us budding pilots, it was very difficult to get adequate simulator time, an important aspect of flying.

As an alternative to the simulator, the cadets were advised to make a scale representation of the cockpit dials and major switches on a chart paper. This was pasted on the wall just across the study table. The diagrams of the horizontal switches and control panels were placed on the table. A hockey stick tethered to the table with string served as the control (joy) stick. Whenever the boys got free time, they were expected to sit in front of this 'simulator' and practise their air and ground procedures.

Some instructors would come over to the rooms in the evening and monitor the progress of their pupils on the room simulator. They would insist that we get used to the 'bone-dome' as well. The bone-dome was essentially a hard outer helmet which protected the soft inner helmet that contained the mike and earphones, attachment for oxygen, and the mask. The valve of the oxygen tube had to be kept open with the help of a matchstick. If you didn't keep it open this way, it was almost impossible to breathe with the mask on your face. In the real aircraft however, the oxygen tube was connected to the oxygen system.

It was quite comical to see the budding pilots in their rooms in their night suits, wearing their helmets and mask, visors covering their faces and hockey stick in hand. Did it really give us a feel of being in the air? Not really. But this training was important. The mask was uncomfortable to say the least and had a typical rubbery smell and this practice got us used to it to a large extent. A large number of us landed up with 'mask bites' before flying actually began. The red vertical welts across the cheeks made us look like Hanuman, the Hindu god, and we were called just that in jest by our friends.

The rookie pilot needs to know the position of each of the switches and dials in the aircraft and be so familiar with them that he could point them out blindfolded. Before flying began, the instructors took the boys to the actual aircraft and practised what were known as 'blindfold checks' over and over again. We all took to this training rather well as it was completely new. We also became conscious that this was serious stuff. One small mistake could lead to catastrophe. It was after all a flying machine and not a scooter or car which one could stop in the middle of the road. Everything about flying was a matter of life and death, we realised.

The day of the first 'gen test' dawned. We had studied through the night and crammed the checklist as well as we could. Now it was time to put pen to paper and reproduce it. MP was one of the 25-odd cadets who passed the exam. The flying was to begin soon. The air of expectation intensified, the adrenalin levels were high.

MP got airborne for his first familiarisation (fam) sortie sometime in the beginning of February 1984. His instructor, Flight Lieutenant 'Muff' Murthy, first took him through a very simple profile to see whether the boy was comfortable inside a platform that moved in all the three planes. He soon realised that MP was, and therefore attempted to take him through a few aerobatic manoeuvres too—the loops, rolls and barrel-rolls. It was like spinning around in an enclosed cage. By the time MP went through the 45-minute profile, he was in a daze, his stomach churning. The instructor asked him if he felt at ease after each manoeuvre. It was like nothing he'd ever imagined. He had 'pulled g' for the first time—thrilling but uncomfortable at the same time.

When one 'pulls g', the blood rushes away from the brain towards the lower extremities of the body, leading to haziness in vision or a blackout, depending on the severity of the manoeuvre. For example, 3G means that you were being acted on by three times the force of gravity; it is difficult to do simple things like talk or lift one's hand during such manoeuvres unless one gets used to it.

All of us were expected to carry a 'puke bag' stuffed into the leg pocket of the overall so that we could ease our churning stomachs if required during the initial sorties. The instructors did not want to get the cockpit messy and ensured we always had a suitably strong bag along. Post landing, as MP walked towards the crew room, he had to rush to the restroom to throw up. He had managed to go through the entire profile without much of a problem.

Later, when he compared notes with others who had gone through similar sorties with their instructors, he realised that he had done pretty well in comparison. Some of the boys had thrown up immediately on getting airborne while some had given up during the aerobatics. 'It is a question of getting used to being inside a small enclosed space, being strapped tight to a seat and being tossed around in space', our instructors told us.

The pace of flying intensified as soon as this introductory phase was over and the cadets were comfortable. There were 85 hours of flying per head to be completed in the next four months. By the time MP reached his solo stage at the 20th sortie, a large number of our friends were already being grounded. While some could not get used to the 'air' environment, others could not cope with control over the airplane. I was lucky to be the lone pupil of my flight commander. He managed to push my pace and I was proud to be the first to go solo in the course.

The number of aeroplanes available on flight line for the course was more or less fixed. Therefore, only a certain amount of flying was available for the course training. That necessarily put a cap on the total number of candidates who could complete this training. The stragglers, late starters or slow learners were grounded. By the end of the first semester of flying, only around 40 of us cadets remained to fly in the second semester.

It was sad to see some of our friends go. But then NDA had taught us the art of survival and we learned to move on. Some of those grounded went either to the ground duty branches of the IAF or simply moved over to the navy or army, losing about six months of seniority in the process. They went on to do very well in their second choice of profession, proving that the NDA cadet is versatile and able to adapt to any environment in life.

Before we flew our first 'solo', there were more hurdles to be cleared. Some 'check' or test sorties were to be flown with the senior instructors who would then clear us to go solo. In the 85 hours we flew at the AFA, we were expected to get a fair idea about the experience of being in the medium of air—'air sense' as it is called. We went through 'general handling' sorties which included aerobatics, followed by navigation and some exposure to instrument flying and night flying.

MP's instructor, 'Muff' Murthy, now retired and flying as a commercial pilot in an airline, describes MP as a sweet, shy and simple rustic boy who preferred to remain in the background but took to the skies as if he was born to be up there. He remarks, 'MP was like a sponge and absorbed all that was taught to him.

Right from the first time he went up, he was comfortable in the cockpit, proving that he would be a good pilot. He displayed good hand-eye coordination while flying the aeroplane'.

During this phase the course saw a couple of ejections. Luckily, the occupants of the aircraft were safe, but the aircraft were wrecks. The first ejection happened in front of my eyes when a solo sortie being flown by Bob Sivaraman had an engine failure over the airfield; he ejected and landed right in front of the Air Traffic Control tower (ATC) across the runway. As fire-fighting and safety teams rushed to the spot, Bob had already collected his parachute and started walking back to the crew room. A bit dazed, he was forced into an ambulance and taken to hospital for a check-up, but he ensured that the parachute was never out of his sight. The parachute and the seat that saves a pilot become his proud property and are often displayed prominently at home. A famous ejection seat manufacturer, Martin Baker, is known to present a diamond tiepin to each pilot saved by their seats.

The second ejection happened far from base. Shankar Krishnamurthy aka 'Shanks' was being introduced to 'spin' in the Kiran at about 20,000 feet by his instructor Flight Lieutenant Stephen. As they tried to recover from the manoeuvre, the aircraft went out of control and continued falling like a leaf. The instructor made Shanks eject first and followed soon after. Both were safe and picked up by a rescue helicopter immediately. While Stephen had a slight back concussion, both Bob Sivaraman and Shanks were back in the cockpit soon, reinforcing our confidence in the safety features of our aeroplane. Before every takeoff in a combat aircraft, the pilot practises the ejection drill, so that, when the time comes to leave a sick aeroplane, there is no delay.

At the end of the first six months of training, our course was split into two groups. One half was to go to Bidar in Karnataka to carry out advanced training on the Kiran Mark-II and the other half moved to fly the Polish jet trainer Iskra at the base at Hakimpet in Secunderabad.

Advanced flying training

HAKIMPET WAS close to the town of Secunderabad and was home to the Helicopter Training School (HTS) and Fighter Training Wing (FTW). With the HT-2 aircraft being phased out, the Iskra (meaning 'spark' in Polish) had been downgraded to become the advanced jet trainer. Hitherto, the aircraft had been used for pre-fighter flying training before pilots graduated to the MiG series of aeroplanes.

MP was chosen to fly the Iskra and he was mighty happy about it. The Polish aircraft was more akin to a fighter—more sleek, with tandem seating compared to the side-by-side seating of the Kiran, and boasted a more modern, fighter-style cockpit. When MP first looked at the machine he was to fly, his heart skipped a beat. It looked and felt just like a fighter. As he went around the machine admiring its sleek features, he thought to himself, 'Just six more months to realise my dream!'

Iskra flying commenced much the same way Kiran flying had at the AFA—the initial phase of ground training, followed by a test, followed then by learning the new checks and procedures. But this time it was easier. The air sense learnt in the first phase had kicked in and everything was falling into place. We now realised that everything about aviation relies on logic. The quantum of flying to be done here was much more than the earlier term and there was no time to lose.

Flying in the advanced stage was more demanding than at AFA. Besides the routine 'general handling' sorties, one had to go solo by night, learn about bombing and rocketry from the aircraft, and some tactical flying like close formation, low-level navigation and combat. Little by little, we were learning to use the aeroplane as a weapon.

At Hakimpet, MP's flying skills came to the fore. He demonstrated smooth and impeccable control over the aircraft, which made him a pet of the chief instructor, Wing Commander A Anukul, popularly known as 'Daddy Cool'. Anukul loved the way MP handled the aeroplane, especially during aerobatics, and often praised MP in front of all the instructors.

We all saw the chief instructor as a role model, secretly hoping that one day we would also manage to impress him with our flying skills. Besides Anukul, our instructors included some famous pilots who had been taken as POWs during the Pakistan conflict but had managed to escape. They had inspirational stories to tell about their war experiences. Many years later, MP did a story on their escape, which sparked off a movement to honour them.

MP was happy at the way things were panning out. But there was a small hitch. If rumours were to be believed, there were to be just four or five vacancies for fighters for the term ending December 1984. The maximum vacancies were to be for helicopters and it was feared that most of the course would be sent to fly choppers after commissioning. So to be selected to fly fighters, one would have to be at the top of the class. MP began working harder.

THE CADETS' mess in Hakimpet was located in old barracks across the runway, quite close to a small village called Yamjal. The cadets were quite independent here, far from the prying eyes of their instructors. The young officers of the HTS, just six months their seniors, also lived at this mess. These young officers were good to have as friends since they were already earning, had motorbikes, and of course, fewer restrictions of staying in camp etc.

On Sundays the bus from Yamjal took the cadets to Secunderabad Railway Station. Here the day was spent watching movies, eating out and generally gallivanting through the busy streets of town. Some keen movie buffs like MP saw three movies back to back.

A few minutes delay at the theatre would mean missing the last bus and trudging home. Then one had to resort to hitch-hiking on trucks, sitting amidst chemicals, oil drums or cattle. The last leg of the journey was a late night walk through the deathly quiet of the villages. Despite their late night sojourns, the cadets were young and strong enough to take on the rigours of flying the next day. Later in life, they would themselves understand the importance of adequate rest prior to a flying day.

The cadets still had to slog their way to work on their ubiquitous bicycles. This ride took them through the village square and a small road led to a runway crossing where one had to wait when flying was in progress. The village had a tea stall which served strong milky tea which the cadets loved to down with hot pakodas, especially on their way back from flying.

Flying was carried out in two shifts. The first shift flew early in the morning and proceeded with their ground training classes from 10 am onwards. The second shift began their flying after an early lunch. It was wonderful to see the aeroplanes with their canopies open and pointing towards the skies all lined up parallel to each other, glistening in the sun. It looked like the war scenes in the commando comics that the boys had been so fond of reading!

On September 8, 1984, MP was in the second shift and waiting along with a bunch of his friends at the runway barrier to cross over after the 'detail' landed. They could see some aircraft taking off and some landing. Suddenly the alarm bell at the ATC sounded and the crash fire tenders shot out of their parking slots and proceeded towards the end of the runway.

Leaning against their cycles, the boys looked at each other and wondered what was wrong. Some discussions on what could have happened ensued. Someone thought it was a tyre burst during landing while someone else conjectured that it was a simulation exercise to test the crash crews. The more curious attempted to climb a tree close by to check it out. Nothing. The barrier continued to be closed and there seemed to be no flying activity. Something was surely wrong.

After what seemed a long time, the gate opened and the boys sped towards the crew room. There was a pall of gloom. 'What happened?' asked someone. 'Bains crashed just after takeoff', came the reply. Has he ejected? Was it a solo? What happened? When? Where? No one had any answers at the time. The instructors were huddled in their crew room and there was a numbing hush around.

Bains had crashed into the nearby Jedimatla Lake, located right next to the runway. All efforts were on to recover him from the aeroplane which had gone under. Some naval divers were also called in. The cadet in his death proved his mettle. As the engine failed just after takeoff at 150 metres above ground, there was no chance of ejection since the seat had a height limitation of 250 metres to function properly. The engine could not be restarted either due to the short time available and the only option was to glide the aircraft away from populated areas and put it down in the nearest clear area, which happened to be the edge of the lake.

Bains managed to glide his aeroplane and put it down on the banks of the lake. As the aircraft slid along the uneven lakeside, it hit a hump, swerved and went into the lake which was about 20 feet deep. Bains had managed to survive the impact of the crash. Under water, he undid his harness and helmet, and opened the canopy to get out of the aeroplane. As he came out, he got entangled in the dense weeds at the bottom of the lake. He then tried to take his shoes off to set himself free. He got further entangled and finally suffocated to death.

MP wrote the story of Bains' courage many years later in the 'Time Out' section of *The Indian Express*. 'The news of his demise cast a pall of gloom on the habitually boisterous aircrew room. Heads drooped. Hearts sank. The grim silence conveyed our collective agony.' As with all fighting forces, it was decided to get on with flying immediately so as to put the episode behind us. He adds, 'It was done to mentally reassure us rookies and to tersely state that life has to go on'.

This was the first fatality of the course and more were lined up for us later. Despite his limited experience, Bains had displayed the highest level of airmanship and possibly saved a number of lives on the ground. I remember my interaction with Bains the night before the accident. He had come to my room to ask for a spare inland letter form to send home. I had a few but had already addressed them. Bains was in a pensive mood and stood outside alone, staring at the full moon. I went and stood next to him. He was a good six foot plus and I had to raise myself on my toes to put a reassuring hand around his shoulders and say I was sorry I couldn't help. This done, we shook hands and headed back to our rooms. So many years on, I often wonder how I could have helped Bains write his last letter home.

Besides this accident, the course went through the training without a hitch. A few guys had to withdraw due to medical or administrative reasons and the course strength kept reducing. Meanwhile the cadets at the advanced course in Bidar went through similar training on the Kiran aircraft, without mishap.

The 'debrief' sessions were held in the evening after flying for the day was done. Often the instructors indulged in a bit of friendly banter with the boys to reduce the tension they operated under: How was your landing? I saw all the villagers running away from their homes when you were on approach!... Were you doing some low-level aerobatics? That was a real bouncer of a landing! You did some dancing on the runway after touchdown... Feeling frisky? You call that an alignment on approach?... It was as if you wanted to crash directly into the crew room!

At the start of flying for the day, one of the instructors would narrate an anecdote and all of us were obliged to laugh even if we didn't find it funny. This was supposed to lighten the atmosphere in the briefing room before the serious stuff began.

Thereafter, one of the instructors would quiz us on a simulated situation; it went something like this:

'You are flying in sector at 25,000 feet; suddenly as you open throttle, you hear a loud bang and the RPM winds down and the jet pipe temperature increases... What is the emergency and what would you do... Flight cadet so and so... please come forward and tell us what action would you take?' It forced us to study for these sessions and be prepared with all the emergency actions at our fingertips. The more prepared we were, the more likely our actions in the air would be prompt and accurate. Once this emergency session was over, the flying programme was read out and we went to our instructors for individual sortie briefs before flying commenced.

It was a life full of tension, but enjoyable too. To cool things down, sometimes, at the end of the day, after debriefs were completed, one of us would be asked to tell a joke or mimic an instructor. Once, it was MP's turn. Without realising that there were four or five Sikh instructors in the audience, MP rattled out, 'Two sardars were playing chess'. It was a short and sweet joke, but mistimed! One of the Sikh instructors asked, 'Was that a joke?' MP smiled innocently and nodded his head. While we guffawed, he was soon measuring the corridors rolling and jumping on his haunches—an activity he hadn't indulged in after leaving NDA. However, the instructors did manage a small private laugh when MP was out of earshot!

Muff Murthy often used to smile to himself when he heard his pupils flying and giving the radio calls in their 'mallu'-style English. He often quipped to those around him, 'There goes my Kerala coconut flying like an unguided missile!'

Commissioning

AT THE end of November 1984, all flying was over and the cadets moved back to the Air Force Academy for the final commissioning parade on December 21, 1984. This parade was to be held along with ground duty counterparts of the course and Air Chief Marshal LM Katre, who had just taken over the reins of the air force in September 1984, was to be the chief guest. The academy was abuzz. We were to get our first stripes, and 38 of us were to receive our flying badges. Incidentally, Air Marshal Katre was to die in office a few months later, on July 1, 1985.

MP's parents again decided against leaving their village to witness the passing out parade. Sheeja says she couldn't convince them to go despite the invitation letter arriving well in time. The commissioning would be celebrated in the old village way, with a feast for friends and relatives. They had no idea that MP was again going to get a special trophy for being best in aerobatics.

The passing out parade at the AFA in those days was not as grand as the one at NDA, but it is here that the cadets get their commission as officers. The parade was followed by a spectacular flypast carried out by our instructors to wish us 'God Speed, Good Luck and Happy Landings'. The foyer of the AFA building has an imposing statue of a pilot in full flying regalia, flying helmet against his hip. 'Through the portals of this academy pass out the best pilots in the world', reads the plaque below.

Another hurdle had been crossed. Flight Cadet Anil Kumar MP was now Pilot Officer Anil Kumar MP; a first class gazetted officer of the Indian Armed Forces.

'Smitten by aircraft, bewitched by flying, fascinated by the frisson of foiling gravity, I joined the IAF', MP wrote many years later.

The commissioned officers were to be 'trifurcated' into three streams—the fighters, transports and helicopters. The rumour about the fewer vacancies for the fighter stream had been true. Only five were to go to fighters, seven to transports and 26 to the helicopter stream. It meant that most of us who had opted for fighters were not to get the stream of our choice. 'Whatever the stream you have been chosen for, remember you are privileged and lucky to be part of the flying fraternity of the IAF', our instructors counselled. 'It is as challenging and difficult to fly any type of aircraft.'

MP, of course, was heading to fly the MiG series of aircraft after a small break at the two squadrons that made up the MOFT (MiG Operational Flying Training) in Tezpur (Assam). He was to be accompanied by four more stalwarts of the course. They were to accompany 14 more pilot officers from our senior course who were finishing their training alongside us in Bidar.

The helicopter chaps were to move to the HTS (Helicopter Training School) and the transport chaps to TTW (Transport Training Wing) in Bangalore. The fighter pilots were being further bifurcated, some to fly the Hunter aircraft of western origin, the rest to fly the Russian ones.

Twenty years after the accident, MP wrote, 'When I look back, the Sainik School, NDA and the fighter cockpit were what made me what I am. The attributes—discipline, composure, alertness, application and, above all, aggression—demanded by the fighter jet from her jockey were sown and nurtured at the Sainik School, NDA and AFA. In one quirky instant 20 years ago, a mishap reduced me to a wreck of a combat pilot. From the fighter cockpit to a wheelchair, from a bird's eye view to a worm's eye view of the world... Life was never the same'.

He ends his piece by saying, 'I shall not dwell on the rebirth it forced upon me, but suffice it to say that I relied on the survival skills I learned and honed at the Sainik School and the NDA to bounce back into the arena of life. The rigorous regimen of the academies made us hardy individuals and prepared us to prevail over adversity'.

Tezpur

TEZPUR IS a small town on the northern banks of the meandering Brahmaputra River which splits the eastern State of Assam longitudinally. Assam and its sister States in the northeast have a large number of airstrips built during British times, especially during World War II when the famous 'Hump' operations took place and the Allied forces captured Burma. Some of these airfields were developed post-independence and provide the much-needed strategic reach and power of the air force.

The Tezpur base was built in 1942 and was used by the United States Air Force (USAF) Tenth Air Force as a B-24 Liberator heavy bomber base. The IAF moved into the base in 1959 and it has been one of the most active bases of the Eastern Air Command since. The base saw operations during the 1962 China conflict as well as during the liberation of Bangladesh in 1971.

In 1985, the base had two training squadrons which were soon to come under one banner called the MiG Operational Flying Training Unit (MOFTU) in 1986. This is where MP landed up in January 1985 as a pilot officer, along with his four course-mates and 14 senior course-mates. Tezpur was a training squadron, and the atmosphere here was very unlike that at operational flying squadrons.

The rookies were to fly the MiG-21 trainer variant called the Type 69/66 and the fighter version called the MiG-21 Type 77 at this base before they were posted to operational fighter squadrons after a year. The Mikoyan Gurevich-21, codenamed 'Fishbed' by NATO, has been one of the most popular fighter designs ever produced. This 'supersonic' jet was capable of beating the speed of sound and at that time was being flown in 60-odd countries across the world.

Although the aircraft first went into production in Russia back in 1956, it was not until 1964 that it was inducted into the IAF. It was not fully operationalised during the war of 1965 and therefore found limited use during this conflict. Lessons learnt during 1965 prompted the IAF to request for more of these machines. Since then, more than 1,200 of these aeroplanes have been inducted into the IAF. Most of them have been decommissioned today after being the frontline fighters for over five decades. An upgrade programme has extended the life of a few of these fighters till 2020 (http://www.bharat-rakshak.com/).

The MiG pilots of the IAF were the only ones who had seen active combat and the classic dog-fights of the 1971 war. The stories of the air-to-air combat and tactics followed to shoot down the acclaimed American F-104s prompted other nations to seek Indian help in training their pilots. More recently, the aircraft was used in the Kargil conflict of 1999. So shrouded in mystery was the aircraft that the US took over the entire MiG fleet of the Indonesian air force for evaluation, soon after they put an anti-communist regime in power in that country in the 1960s.

The newly commissioned officers bristled with pride at being able to fly the most sought-after fighter aeroplane in the world. Before they got into the cockpit, they had to go through a month-long ground training to master the innards of the machine as well as checks and procedures. The MiG was a wonderful machine to fly but it was unforgiving too. 'One had to learn to respect the limitations of the aircraft and then enjoy its agility and manoeuvrability', says a veteran MiG pilot. 'It was a difficult and daunting task, both for the trainees and the instructors, primarily because of the almost double jump in speed from the jet trainer like the Kiran and Iskra to the MiG', writes another MiG pilot, now retired.

Tezpur was hot, wet and musty. The long monsoon periods meant that time for flying training was restricted. A lot needed to be learnt in that one year. Most importantly, this was the time to hone mental skills and get accustomed to using the machine as a weapon, imbibing the killer instinct. It is this instinct that makes the military pilot different from the others; and this becomes part of every pilot's psyche—even outside of his aircraft.

The instructors told the young officers, 'This is the last time you will be formally taught the nuances of fighter flying. Now you have to learn to use the machine as a weapon of war. In the squadrons, you will have to use your own initiative to learn as much as you can—no one will spoon-feed you anymore'. MP did as much as he could to learn from his instructors now, realising that some of the most important aspects of learning were to absorb what was not taught. The freshers needed to absorb the instructor's psyche. This unstructured training is what would be handed down the generations.

The first pay cheques started to warm the bank accounts of the youngsters. MP was prompt in sending a major part of his salary to his parents. The money had to be wired and took a while to reach the southern corner of the country from the northeast.

Most of the boys had now acquired motorcycles and outings on these were fun. Tezpur is located quite close to the elephant reserves of the Kaziranga National Park to its south and the high hills of the Tawang sector of Arunachal Pradesh to the north. Both these could be visited on long weekends or short spells of leave and provided the much-needed rest and recuperation.

MP took to playing some serious squash. He was taught the game by his schoolmate and one course senior OM Nirmal Kumar. MP quickly became the champion of the air force base, to the consternation of Nirmal. When the senior course was posted to operational units after the first six months, our course became the senior course in charge of the new lot of juniors who came in. Most of them knew each other from the NDA days and the newcomers were given unofficial training by the senior course.

One of MP's friends from NDA was Vikram (name changed on request). He was one of the toppers of his course and he and his friends were ready to absorb everything that was thrown at them. Vikram was very close to MP from the NDA days and MP took the young man under his wing, teaching him all that was to be taught outside of the cockpit.

'For us youngsters, it was very helpful to have a mentor like MP Anil Kumar', Vikram wrote to me. 'From preparation for sorties to dealing with the room bearers (orderlies as they were called), MP covered a lot of ground in helping us settle in. He was as active in teaching us the mores of social interaction in the squadron... A few things taught by MP will stay with me forever. The tricks to survival in the squadron included avoiding too many additional duties.' MP advised the youngsters to walk around the squadron, files in hand, looking harried and stressed out. The flight commander or instructors would avoid giving these 'busy' officers any more duties! 'This formula really worked and it was christened "Look Busy Do Nothing" or LBDN in short.' He further writes, 'How to arrange the bar and plan and execute the food and entertainment part of social functions was also taught to us by MP. He believed in hands-on instruction through demonstration. As we got the hang of things he let us go solo in the activity. All that MP taught me in the first year at Tezpur has stood me in good stead through the decades; MP was truly a remarkable man'.

Speaking to his juniors about the MiG-21, MP often said, 'The MiG-21 is a real gem; but she is unforgiving if pushed beyond the envelope. All flying machines have kinks and this aeroplane is no different. But you guys must learn to follow the rulebook and exploit the potential of the aircraft, staying within the parameters defined'. MP was dead right. The MiG-21 had been designed by the Russians to intercept the high-flying U-2 flown by the Americans and was never designed for combat as such. Due to its freak design, it was exploited by air forces the world over for a multitude of 'fighter' tasks.

Tezpur had squadrons to train the rookies on the oldest variant of the MiG-21, the Type-77. MP was initially posted in 30 Sqn. He got on the wrong side of the Commanding Officer of his unit over a trivial incident. One thing led to another. Differences crept in on the social and professional front.

Group Captain Raghavan (Rags) was one of the instructors posted to the No 8 'Pursoots' Squadron. A Flight Lieutenant at the time and a bachelor, he lived along with the 40-odd Pilot Officers in the Officers' Mess and was quite close to MP. He remembers MP as a quiet youngster flying with the 'Rhinos' (No 30 Sqn) who had a wry sense of humour and a questioning mind. Raghavan writes, 'A few months after the incident with the CO, MP had reached the second phase of flying called the tactical phase. Here he was expected to manoeuvre his aircraft in relation to another and also had to practise "station keeping" (keeping the position constant in relation to the other) during these manoeuvres'.

In this phase, the CO found him lacking in flying skills. He continues, 'The situation reached crisis proportions when a training review board (TRB) was ordered to see if he was to continue his training in fighters'. In the opinion of the CO of the squadron, MP was unfit to continue. The CO of Pursoots was now asked to do an independent evaluation.

Raghavan continues, 'It was discovered that the problem was not so much in Anil's flying ability but with what was referred to as an "attitudinal deficiency". He had questioned the veracity of certain briefings and statements which was considered insubordination by his CO and seniors'. He adds, 'A Pilot Officer questioning a Wing Commander and Squadron Leader? Unheard of!'

The CO of the Pursoots realised that Anil was a competent pilot and came up with a neat solution. Anil was to be transferred to Pursoots and his progress monitored by the new boss himself. The decision regarding his future in flying would be taken after evaluation under the new CO. So one fine day in July 1985, MP changed from being a Rhino to a Pursoot. The first sortie for evaluation was to be flown by none other than Raghavan!

In one of his mails to me Raghavan writes, 'Of course, almost all of us knew from the outset that Anil wasn't what he was made out to be. That sortie and many others, where I led him through different manoeuvres and taught him a few tricks on the MiG-21, went rather smoothly and Anil turned out to be a good trainee. He still had this little penchant to get a little too involved in the whys and wherefores of many of the tactics and capabilities of the aircraft'. Whenever his questioning attitude got out of hand, many of the instructors would gently ask Anil if he wanted to become a Rhino again—that would shut him up! He ends, 'Anil was one of the best wingmen I have ever had.... solid in his flying and dependable as a No 2 in my formation'. One often wonders where Anil would have been posted had he not changed his squadron in Tezpur. All the pilots from 30 Sqn eventually went on to fly the higher version of the MiG and if MP had been there, he would have been flying the MiG-27 or the 29 and may not have been posted to Pathankot at all.... One can only wonder at the possibilities now...That transfer of squadron turned out to be a turning point in his life in retrospect.

Though Anil was five years junior to Raghavan, an inexplicable bond was established between the two 'Injuns' (as they were called at NDA) in Tezpur. 'My formation call sign was Spitfire-1 and whoever flew as my wingman was Spitfire-2', Raghavan writes. 'Anil and his friend OM Nirmal Kumar decided to play with me and my call sign whenever they flew as wingmen to me. Before starting for a sortie, there was a mandatory radio communication check between aircraft. As I announced "Spitfire Check" on the radio, my wingmen were supposed to reply, "Spitfire-2!" Anil and Nirmal always replied "Spitfire-Thhoo" pronounced in that manner for effect! Apart from taking the obvious dig at the literal meaning of my call sign, they were also referring to my being rather short-tempered those days, especially with non-performers. It took some gumption to do that, as rookies!'

Writing after his death, in September 2014, Raghavan says, 'Rest in peace my friend; so many of us have been inspired by your sheer doggedness, to never give up, in one of the worst situations of adversity that man can ever be faced with. For me, you will always be my good wingman who forever pulled my leg on RT with your Spitfire Thhooo!'

December 1985 brought an end to another phase in Anil's life. It was time to move to operational squadrons. The posting orders arrived and MP was slated to go to No 3 Squadron at Pathankot which was equipped with the MiG 21 'BIS' at that time.

Pathankot

NO 3 SQUADRON, Indian Air Force, January 1986. MP travelled a long way from Trivandrum after a four-week break at home to become part of one of the oldest squadrons of the IAF.

The 'Cobra' family welcomed Anil with the usual prank. He was bundled into the flight commander's office and informed that he had arrived a week late and that severe disciplinary action had been initiated for the lapse. 'You are likely to be stripped of your rank since you are still on probation', they told him.

The masquerading flight commander was one of the senior Flight Lieutenants. MP was now marched up to his supposed CO's office where another officer posed as a foul-mouthed boss. The actual CO and flight commander played their roles as airmen who sympathised with MP and filled him with information on how bad the squadron was and how they were sick and tired of their painful boss. MP was a little flustered but played along, suspecting that something was amiss.

The joke finally ended in the evening where he was welcomed with a cocktail organised at the officers' mess. After much backslapping and guffawing, he was now a newborn Cobra.

No 3 Squadron had a rich heritage and history. Formed in Peshawar in 1941, the squadron had seen operations in Pakistan as well as the Burma campaign before it was handed over to the IAF post-Partition. After Independence, the Tempests and Spitfires formed part of the equipment of the squadron and took part in the operations against the Nizam of Hyderabad. Over time, Vampires replaced these machines for a short duration after which the Dassault Ouragans and finally the jets arrived in 1958 in the form of the Mysteres (bharatrakshak.com).

The squadron first saw major action in the 1965 conflict with Pakistan and was responsible for the famous sabre kills when they adopted the special 'sabre baiting' missions conceived by its pilots. They continued to fly the Mystere and hone their skills in the intervening period till the 1971 conflict, when the squadron operated these aircraft one last time before converting to the MiG-21 in 1972.

Squadron Leader Sumit Mukherjee was the flight commander of the unit when MP joined. In an email to me he reminisces, 'On first impression Anil came across as a very bright boy, a quick learner... He would query and want details about the whys and hows of whatever was taught to him. It indicated to me a keenness to imbibe professional knowledge and build strong foundations. He was always up-to-date and conscientious about taking notes and studying in his own time. We were brought up in pretty much the same way and it was nice to see someone following the same path'.

One bright crisp morning, soon after his arrival, it was decided to send MP on duty to Leh, located at 11,500 feet. He had hardly settled down to the cold conditions of Punjab and was now going to sub-zero temperatures. He was excited at the prospect of seeing snow for the first time in his life. He was to train to become a Forward Air Controller (FAC) and learn to control fighters on to their targets in war. He writes, 'As I was about to catch an An-32 (Antonov-32) flight to Leh, my deputy flight commander took me aside and launched into a monologue on the need to acclimatise to the high altitudes of Leh, Thoise and Siachen. I could not figure out why he was wasting his breath about acclimatisation to a red-blooded, supremely fit 21-year-old. In one ear and out the other, I dismissed his counsel'.

He arrived in the biting cold of Leh in the afternoon, having had an aerial look at the snow-capped Himalayan ranges for the first time in his life. He stood outside his room in the officers' mess, his eyes feasting on the beauty and freshness of the place when young Flight Lieutenant Kharb approached him. 'Would you like to join me for some hill climbing?' He pointed towards the southwest and said, 'Can you see the Spituk Monastery and the hill behind? We will climb that!'

'Righto!' said MP and followed him excitedly up the hill. 'As we reached the Gompa situated halfway, I was panting and in dire need of oxygen; my heart beat very fast, as if I had run a marathon. Severe breathlessness soon forced me on to my haunches first and then my bum.' As he recouped, two words kept resounding in his ears: altitude and acclimatisation! He continues, 'This rude, practical lesson in high altitude sickness humbled my brashness, and taught me the hard way to respect the elements, and wise counsel. Above 10,000 feet the human body needs to get accustomed to the lower oxygen content, and the higher you go, the longer the body takes to adapt'.

From Leh, Anil had the unique opportunity to visit the highest battlefield in the world—the Siachen Glacier. Here he understood how the Indian army and IAF operate at high altitudes in a warlike situation. He looked at the men in greens with awe; these men risked life and limb to guard our frontiers round the clock, through blizzards and extremes of weather. He also had a firsthand look at helicopter operations that were being carried out in support of these ground forces and understood the hazards of flying in this glaciated region.

Baptised by fire, MP stayed in the Leh area for almost a month, thoroughly enjoying his time in the cold before returning to Pathankot. He went to the deputy's office and told him about the hill climbing experience at Leh. The deputy grinned at him with a 'told you so' look and said, 'We generally don't learn from others' mistakes, do we?' This was another important lesson to the strong-willed young man.

Speaking of MP's flying abilities, Mukherjee says, 'His flying abilities were above average and we were happy to see him contributing to the operational capability of the squadron at such a young age'. Mukherjee was posted out to attend a course in September '86 but he was back in the squadron when the red alert was sounded during Exercise 'Brass Tacks'. War clouds loomed and it was time to prepare for the ultimate test. 'The youngsters got themselves fully involved in getting the camouflage paint on to the aircraft and getting them ready in the required configurations.'

He writes about MP running around getting the communication lines going, his overalls smeared in green, brown and yellow paint. 'The youngsters displayed tremendous dedication, spent sleepless nights and devoted themselves to whatever task they were entrusted with', he says proudly.

MP writes, 'The MiG-21 was a marvellous aeroplane. The sheer brute force and the trembling of the earth beneath your feet with full afterburner while rolling for takeoff... Ahh! It was absolutely awesome! Actually if you look at it objectively, without bias, this machine is the best-looking fighter aeroplane of its time. There was plenty of experience and good grooming available in the squadron, and at no time did we feel scared or intimidated by the machine or its flying characteristics. We were taught to respect its nuances, study its aerodynamics and feel it reaching the limits of its flight envelope by the seat of our pants'. The most important point drilled into every pilot's head was never to get overconfident or take it easy. Anil followed the instructions to the letter and over the next two years, he had become a thorough fighter pilot in all respects. He was over the moon when he was chosen to run for the 'Best Upcoming Fighter Pilot' trophy, a coveted honour. Alas, the accident played spoilsport and this remained just a dream.

In January 1987, there was a crash in Pathankot that MP wrote about many years later. Flight Lieutenant Ranbir Singh 'Bira' crashed during a tactical training sortie near the base. He was No 2 to the senior flight commander Squadron Leader 'Kid' Mehta. He managed to eject just in time and the aircraft was blown to smithereens. Mukherjee remembers how he rushed on a rescue helicopter to the crash site and went out looking for Bira.

The gutsy fellow was luckily not injured and he managed to hitch a lift on a cycle, parachute clutched to his chest, to the nearest village hospital. Mukherjee was directed to this hospital by a villager at the crash site and was relieved to see the young man all in one piece. Bira was taken through the usual medical check-up and after a brief sabbatical, was back in the cockpit. MP was there to look after him in the hospital and run errands to make him comfortable, he remembers fondly. At the end of the article, MP writes, 'Happy birthday, Bira! Bira still celebrates his second birth every year as his additional birthday'.

LIFE AT an operational fighter squadron called for three important qualities the youngsters learnt. In the cockpit one had to be a thorough professional—correct, quick and ruthless. In the squadron one had to be part of a large family, understanding relationships, being compassionate and working towards common goals without thinking of one's own. And at home one had to be a 'jazz' person—happy go lucky, fun-loving, wild and naughty and living life to the fullest. The common thread, I have always believed, is to be a good human being; everything else drops into place.

The squadron had an active social life. It was important to bond socially so that one could fly and fight alongside. The duty of the flight commander and CO was to bind the squadron into one well-knit family. There were always birthdays and anniversaries being celebrated. MP was not very comfortable with drinking. 'He used to have a tot or two once in a while and that too quite reluctantly', says a friend. He was shy and reserved in the company of the squadron ladies, quite at a loss what to say. One thing was drilled into the youngsters—never talk about flying and work in front of the ladies! He saw and learnt quickly. Very soon the shy boy from the village was one of the most popular amongst the ladies. They were impressed with his wit and sense of humour. He could talk about varied topics with a depth of knowledge. By and by the boy who was rooted in the Malayali culture also learnt to appreciate Hindi and Western music.

The squadron had a tradition of 'bouncing' in those times. Bouncing simply meant that a gang of people descended on a married officer's home unannounced and made the lady cook up a meal while they polished off the liquor in the house. The bouncers almost always played some pranks and there was a lot of noise and laughter late into the night. This was generally done on long weekends so that one could recuperate after late-night binging. The house would be left as if a whirlwind had passed through it. The number of times one got bounced was a rough indicator of one's popularity in the squadron.

On MP's birthday, May 4 midnight, the rest of the squadron landed up at his room. A flustered MP got out of bed, and found himself staring at many freshly baked and iced cakes. A few days later, MP invited the whole squadron for a party in the mess. 'It is so good to be loved and be part of the family of the Cobras', smiled MP to himself as he fell off to sleep.

Every month, MP dutifully sent a money order to his father, along with a letter. He was aware of the various functions that were happening in his hometown and often instructed his father on monetary matters. He had advice for his younger siblings and asked how his pets were doing.

But time had to be finely balanced between fun, frolic and work. Tests and exams are part and parcel of a pilot's life. The system forces you to be a thorough professional. You have to keep abreast of the latest in the field of aviation and also brush up technical knowledge from time to time. Then there were tests of flying skills, with missions to prepare for and fly.

There was fierce competition with the sister squadron at base, be it in flying, inspections, games or even social life. The youngsters on both sides were good friends but when it came to competition, the rivalry surfaced. It was just like in school and NDA—one had to live and die for the honour of the squadron! I remember MP telling me, 'We even competed with each other on who would stay longer at the bar on a Saturday afternoon. Beer sessions would start around 1400 and culminate in lunch as late as 1700 hours. Then there would be a break for a game of squash or a run to get the beer out of the system; a quick shower and the guys would be back at the bar by around 8 pm. Some capacity our young friends had!'

Besides the individual games, matches were often organised at the station level where teams vied for the overall games trophy. With his affinity for games, MP was soon playing in all the squadron teams and enjoying the appreciation of his men. It was so good to play shoulder to shoulder with his juniors; his men also looked up to this young officer. Very soon MP had established himself in his squadron—in the cockpit, at the office and socially. He was adept and fully confident of handling the aeroplane and established a beautiful bond with the machine. He was leading formations and also learning to lead his men on the ground.

Well ensconced in the life of his squadron and almost three years into his tenure, it was time to move on posting. MP was slated to move to No 4 Squadron, flying the same machine. But there was still time to move out of station. One newly produced aircraft had to be ferried from Ojhar near Nashik. MP was selected to go and bring it in.

He was excited to take on the task. He was to go by a commercial flight to Mumbai and then to Ojhar in a taxi. He got down to planning for the trip. The relevant maps were taken and the lines drawn for the route, the bags packed for the short stay and orders and instructions studied in detail. On June 1, 1988, Anil left Pathankot for Ojhar.

Tailspin, and recovery

JULY 15, 1988, Kirkee, or Khadki as the Puneites call it. MP arrived by a special aircraft from Delhi, with doctors in attendance. He was still in and out of consciousness, oblivious to what was happening to him. He was shifted into the special spinal injury ward located near the ICU where the best of care was available.

Kirkee is a small cantonment of British times, tucked away in a rocky part of north-western Pune. It has an old military hospital (MH) which was known as the 7 Indo British General Hospital (IBGH) when it was established to look after battle casualties of the Second World War. Post-Independence, in 1949, it came to be known as MH Kirkee. A special spinal cord injury centre was established here soon after—the first of its kind in India. Today, it is the third largest military hospital in the country and boasts of the largest orthopaedic centre of the armed forces and the largest spinal cord injury centre in southeast Asia. Despite its old and dilapidated look, the hospital was well-known for its orthopaedic and neurological care, with the best of specialists from the armed forces posted here. While the hospital today sports a new and modern building, in 1988, when MP was flown in from Delhi, it was sprawled over numerous old barracks cocooned by shady old trees.

Just behind the hospital complex, almost connected to the hospital, is the Queen Mary Technical Institute (QMTI) and the Paraplegic Rehabilitation Centre (PRC), which together form a unique rehabilitation complex for spinal cord injury patients of the armed forces. Jacob Tharakan, another of MP's schoolmates serving in the army, writes, 'MH Kirkee surgical ward is not meant for the faint-hearted. It is a super-specialty facility for orthopaedic treatment. It is common to find hands and legs suspended at different angles and heights. The groans or cries that frequently erupt can unsettle most'.

While MP had got used to his new environment and was stable, the Commandant and senior doctors contemplated the future course of action. More than physical recovery, mental and psychological recovery was prioritised. There was little hope that MP would ever walk or sit again. Some of the doctors opined that the case was hopeless and it was just a matter of time before the patient succumbed to multi-organ failure resulting from the spinal injury.

MP's brother Jayakumar arrived from Chirayinkeezhu along with other relatives. Although they were completely shocked to see MP in this condition, they hid their feelings when they went in to meet him for the first time.

Quadriplegia

BEFORE WE move on with the story of MP's rehabilitation and the first two years at MH Kirkee, it is important to understand various aspects of spinal cord injury (SCI), especially quadriplegia.

Paralysis of the hands and legs is traditionally termed quadriplegia. 'Quad' comes from Latin meaning 'four' and 'plegia' is borrowed from Greek, meaning 'inability to move'. Today quadriplegia is often referred to as tetraplegia, where both words are taken from Greek. Quadriplegia generally results when a spinal injury occurs near the top of the spine as in MP's case.

'Paraplegia' on the other hand, is the impairment of motor or sensory function of the lower extremities following damage to nervous tissue in a spinal cord injury. In this case, the injury to the nerves could be either in the lumbar, thoracic or sacral regions. If only one limb is affected, the term used is 'monoplegia'.

The entire body is controlled by the brain through the nervous system, a system which remains a medical mystery to date. The system can be simply described as an electric circuitry that runs from the brain to the organs it controls. The motor controls originate at the base of the skull in what is known as the cerebrum and a feedback is received through the same medium from the various sensory organs. These bundles of wires or nerves emerge from the brain and travel through the spinal column to different parts of the body. Since the nerves are ensconced in the vertebrae, they are well-protected from external injury.

In a spinal cord injury, the cord is not actually cut. It is the fibrous extension of the nerve tissue that is crushed or damaged. This causes a 'short circuit' in the hundreds of wires passing through the neck that control different organs. Due to a disruption of the electrical pathways, the person loses sensation and control over various body functions. In Anil's case, the broken pieces of vertebrae disrupted the nerves in the neck where the bundle of nerves is thickest.

Damage to the spinal nerves causes swelling and inflammation, leading to a further disruption of the nervous system. The first action that is taken in a spinal injury is to give medication to control the swelling and to put the person in traction so that the vertebrae are stretched, relieving the pressure on the spinal cord lesion. The patient's neck is kept immobile so that no further aggravation of the nervous tissue occurs when an attempt is made to move the neck.

Although the body is paralysed, there is a considerable degree of pain felt by the body when the muscular tissue tries to send feedback to the erroneous signals it receives due to the short circuit. This sends the hands and legs into spasm and excruciating pain is felt within the body. These are called 'phantom pains'. All this was happening to MP from the time he was moved from the accident site to the local SSQ and then to the military hospitals.

The level of disability and pain differs from case to case and it is said that no two cases of paraplegia or quadriplegia are the same. More importantly, since the recovery is more mental than anything else, treatment must also be individualised. So, it is occupational therapists and physiotherapists who are more useful to these patients than neurophysicians.

The regeneration of the spinal cord has been considered impossible by doctors till very recently. In modern-day medicine, stem cell research has tried to regenerate these cells, with partial success. In 2010, a Polish man named Derek Fidyka suffered spinal injuries in a knife attack and became a quadriplegic. In 2014, he agreed to undergo pioneering spinal surgery of grafting 'olfactory sheathing cells' taken from his brain and grown in a lab. These were then injected above and below the injured spinal tissue. Fidyka regained sensory and motor function in his lower limbs, becoming the world's first partially successful case of recovery of motor and sensory function after severe spinal cord injury. It is hoped that further breakthroughs will solve the mystery of the nervous system.

The first problem that occurs in an SCI case is difficulty in breathing. This happens because the diaphragm is not able to contract and expand involuntarily. A pacemaker is generally inserted in the diaphragm to excite it to contract and expand so that exhalation and inhalation become an involuntary process again. Anil started having breathing problems as soon as he was rushed to MH Pathankot. A tube was inserted into his lungs to help him breathe. He was put on a ventilator. It was several days before he could breathe on his own. It was important to keep him in controlled temperatures and clean surroundings to prevent any lung infection, which would rapidly deteriorate into pneumonia.

In the initial days of rehabilitation at the MH, MP could not be moved much. Lying in one position for long periods, he developed a large number of bedsores. These became ugly infections, which required constant cleaning and medication. Later, as these were controlled and his condition became more stable, the attendants would turn him around every 30 minutes, a practice that he insisted on all his life. Loss of bladder control is another common problem with quadriplegics. Without proper management, this often leads to urinary tract infections (UTIs), which can prove fatal if not treated in time. He was therefore catheterised.

With long periods of immobility, MP's blood circulation was in danger of slowing down, leading to clot formation and further seizures. This was avoided by blood-thinning medicines like aspirin administered daily. There is also a danger of the circulatory system going into shock in such patients. The lack of nervous control can lead to large variations of blood pressure and heart rate and these have to be constantly monitored and managed.

The list of 'likely failures' is endless. '*Any organ can fail anytime*', said a doctor friend, adding, 'The patient has to be kept under close observation all the time'. That is why MP was required to convalesce inside an intensive care unit for the first few months. The ICU, despite its controlled environment, is a place where the maximum number of hospital infections lurk, and therefore all possible hygiene measures are adopted.

The worst, without doubt, is the fact that such patients are mentally and psychologically so beaten that they would prefer to give up their lives than live with these debilities.

A close cousin, Joy, who arrived with Jayakumar to look after Anil sometime in the middle of July 1988, stayed with him for 16 months without a break. 'Anil had 42 stitches along his spine after his surgery and the bedsores were unimaginable', he remembers. 'His back was like rotten jackfruit. It was quite a horrific task to clean the wounds and apply medicines—a task that left us mentally exhausted.'

It was now that MP, his friends and family tried every cure imaginable—from tantriks to soothsayers and from ayurveda to homoeopathy. The religious offered special prayers. By this time, MP had found the will to live and he was desperate to find a solution to his problem, asking his cousins to find all the literature possible for him to read. There seemed to be no light at the end of the tunnel. Desperation turned to despair and MP was an emotional wreck, completely at a loss what to do next. He realised that he was maimed for life. He waited for the doctors to break the news to him officially. He still held on to a tiny glimmer of hope.

When the doctors did tell him the extent of the damage to his nervous system, that last glimmer faded and he was completely devastated. He tried to put up a brave front, but Joy remembers MP saying, 'If I could move my hand, I would have shot myself. What's the point in living in this vegetative state? You take care of Amma; I can't even kill a mosquito...'

What use am I, he wondered, if I cannot even get up and sit in bed? I cannot flick through TV channels or pick up the phone when it rings. I won't ever be able to hug my mother and sisters, ride my motorcycle, or sit in the cockpit, apply reheat and pelt down the runway... This is total helplessness. I am already all but dead, but I need help even to survive like this... Can someone get me a gun? But who will pull the trigger?

Anil lapsed into a long silence over the next few days, but limped back, surrendering to the truth.

Anger followed despair. The normally reserved boy became volatile. Why am I being kept alive, why shouldn't I be allowed to die, he asked the doctors and nurses, rather than making so many people suffer when I am no good to man or beast.

Almost a decade later, in an article published on *rediff.com* in 1997, MP describes those first dark years after the accident, and the experience of the disabled in India. He writes, 'The crippling quirk of fate has severely curbed my wanderlust. However, on the few occasions that I have ventured out, the sight of my decrepit body being wheeled around in a wheelchair seemed to attract undue attention; oftentimes, the curious stares I drew from the onlookers were the kind that are generally reserved for a celebrated escapee from the local zoo than a human being. Well, I am not that ugly! The less said about the unfeigned unconcern of society and the unavailability of civic facilities for the wheelchair-bound, like ramps, wide doors etc at public places, the better. Obviously, our penny wise and pound foolish system is more interested in doling out fake sops than providing the needy with real facilities'.

Severely disabled persons have no choice, MP says, but to accept the world's insensitivity. 'One can fight the encumbrances caused by severe disability, but it is impossible to fight the iniquities and hurdles heaped on them by an insensate society.' Rehabilitation, the catch-all mantra chanted by the government, means more than just equipping the disabled with crutches, prostheses or wheelchairs, he writes. Livelihoods are the key, not handouts. 'The disabled community will be empowered when the support apparatus facilitates them to stand on their own feet, on their own steam', he writes.

He argues that euthanasia should be legalised since it would be consistent with disability rights and would be in the larger interests of society: 'People with disabilities comprise a wide and diverse spectrum of religious and philosophical beliefs. Even with the legal option of ending one's unmitigated suffering, people will find stronger reasons—ethical, religious or personal—not to pursue this option. If we legally allow the few who choose to die quietly, we can then concentrate our energies on addressing the needs of many who choose to live.'

COUNSELLING IS very important for any patient with a debility that has completely altered his or her life. Some people go to professional counsellors, some turn to religion, some just rely on friends. Although some professional counsellors met MP and spoke to him for hours in the beginning, they realised that what he really needed was love and care. It was a very hard time for MP and those around him. He had always been obstinate and now it was difficult to convince him that he had a life ahead and there was a lot that he could still do.

The doctors and nurses tried to boost his morale, but MP continued to be agitated, the despair and anger bubbling over. It required an extraordinary intervention from a special person to get him back on track. She came like an angel into MP's life.

She would like to stay anonymous so we shall call her Sarah. Sarah was a sweet nurse working at the ward. Something about the agitated patient made her go beyond the call of duty. Only a few of MP's friends and MP himself knew what magic she worked on him. It was she who pushed MP to live, and live with purpose.

She offered him unstinted love and care, which was exactly what he needed and longed for at the time. As their interactions continued, she became more and more close to MP. Long discussions about life ensued and soon they knew every aspect of each other's life. There was so much to talk about and discuss now. He looked forward to her company and for the first time since the accident he began to smile when she was near him. She became his confidante and friend. MP saw a spark in her that ignited his own quest for life. He would wait for her to come and everybody noticed how his mood swung when she walked into the ICU.

Love blossomed; it had to, they had so much in common. They kept it a closely guarded secret. In time, a few close friends came to know what was happening and they were extremely happy for MP. MP's closest senior Group Captain PI Murlidharan aka Murli writes, 'He told me about someone special in his life. I hoped that he would settle down with her and have a happy life—or what was left of it'. Things began to look positive; he began to think about living rather than dying. MP would spend hours discussing all sorts of things with Sarah, speaking in his chaste Malayalam. Sarah listened intently, and made sure MP saw the positive side of his life from then on. It was a slow and laborious recovery.

When she was around, however, MP would behave like a spoilt child. He would complain about his diet, medicines, bed, posture, and the smells in the room. He wanted to be taken out of the ICU at the earliest. Sarah was there, even in her off-duty hours, to see that Anil had his food and medicines without throwing tantrums. She was patient and loving and the care in her eyes melted the rage in her patient.

Though not much data is available on MP's road to recovery in those first two years at MH Kirkee, I have put together the story after interacting with many people who were in touch with him in those trying years. I am grateful to them for sharing their memories and interactions.

MP learnt to take one day at a time, to live moment to moment. Mind control, he realised, was the key to survival. He summoned up all the lessons of his training at the academies, all the mental and physical discipline that teaches cadets to confront challenges with strength of mind.

Again and again the question 'Why me?' would flash through his mind. What if there had been a red light on that barrier? What if it hadn't rained that night? What if the power failure hadn't plunged the base into darkness? What if the guard had not lowered the gate to lift it out of the catch?

Slowly and painfully he learnt that the answer lay in dispelling these questions as soon as they appeared. He learnt to let the angry questions subside, and get a move on. MP once told me, 'There are so many times when people innocuously extend their hands in greeting. Besides the discomfort it causes the visitor, I too seethe within. But I just smile at them'. Over time, MP was able to laugh off such situations, adroitly turning the topic to something else without embarrassing the red-faced visitor.

ALL THIS while, MP had been lying supine in bed. For months all he had been seeing was the ceiling and faces peering down at him. Some efforts had been made to make him sit upright but this would lead to nausea and breathlessness, forcing him to be laid back again. With time, he learnt to sit up for about 10 minutes at a time. He learnt how to control his breathing and orient his vestibular canals to make his brain understand the sitting position. By early 1989, MP was able to sit for an hour or two without much anguish. He could now sit up and face people, eat more comfortably and look around. This modicum of contact with the world around him itself led to a faster recovery and soon he was ready to be put in a wheelchair for a 'walk' in the corridors of the barracks.

He was lifted and set up inside the chair like a baby, his torso strapped to the backrest with soft cloth belts. While he sat on a small inflated tube from a scooter tyre, his legs were arranged to fold into the flaps of the foothold of the chair and his hands were placed in his lap. This ensured that the weight of the upper torso was balanced on his lower body through his hands. Now MP was able to see life outside the confines of his room. As he was slowly wheeled around the ward, his eyes soaked in everything and at the end of the 15-minute exercise, he was exhausted but happy. Thus began another major life change.

Muscular atrophy was another problem. Paralysis leads to the disuse of muscles that hold the bones together and aid movement. It literally means 'wastage' or atrophy of the muscles, with muscle mass being lost over time, and the deposit of fat and fibrous tissue in its place. What MP experienced is termed 'denervation and disuse atrophy'. Nothing could be done, except for massage therapy to delay the onset. Various oils were used as recommended by many who cared but it was just a matter of time before the hands and legs curled up and contorted. Some suggested alternative therapies like ayurveda and homeopathy and others suggested faith healers. He tried everything, but the degeneration continued, slow and steady. His body was withering away.

Meanwhile, a steady stream of visitors from his village continued. A support system seemed to have been formed between the Malayali families in Pune and the village far south. These families provided hospitality to the rustic people who came to visit MP, making them comfortable in a far-off, alien city. Sheeja writes about her paternal uncles Devadas and Viswadas who, along with cousins from the army, Asokan and Dinamani, visited MP on numerous occasions. When they returned to the village, the entire clan would gather around and hear about MP's progress.

At home, MP's family prayed and rallied around. Sheeja writes, 'My father's two brothers and sisters came everyday in the evening to be with the family for many months in support of Amma who grieved and cried all the time. A cousin working in the telephone exchange was provided the contact details of people in Pathankot, Delhi and Pune, and he would get whatever news he could to the family'.

Sheeja decided that she wouldn't go to meet her brother in Pune since she wanted to live with her pleasant and happy memories of Anil. In 1990, MP's first mouth-written letter arrived. Acchan and Amma smiled for the first time after the accident. Acchan went around the village showing the letter to everyone until it was in tatters. On receipt of the letter, Sheeja writes, 'we heard the sound of wings flapping. The broken wings of my parents began to flutter'. She continues, 'We have to change ourselves to absorb grief. I kept my grief condensed inside of me and transformed it into kinetic energy, becoming an activist'.

At the squadron in Pathankot, MP was badly missed. Someone or the other was being sent to Pune on a regular basis, to be with Anil for support and feedback from the doctors. Someone ensured that Anil's pay package reached him in time and an account was opened in Kirkee for him. Senior officers including the then chief of air staff, Air Marshal NC Suri and the Air Officers Commanding at Pune, Air Commodore S Krishnaswamy and Air Commodore NAK Browne (both later to become Chief of Air Staff) were in constant touch to follow-up on MP's progress. This organisational support was critical for MP, and the family was assured that he was being looked after as best possible. In fact, MP's rehabilitation at the paraplegic home was a result of the intervention of senior air force and army officers.

Anil's will to survive grew over the months. He was learning to think about the future. Sarah was the centre of his life. She would sit next to his bed and chat endlessly. She seemed to be totally committed to ensuring Anil's recovery now.

Mouth-writing

IT WAS around this time that another lady came into MP's life. We shall call her Josie since she too prefers to remain anonymous. She was the one who first mooted the idea of Anil writing with his mouth. Initially, he laughed it away as an impossibility, but Sarah egged him on to try. At the time there were three quadriplegics at the paraplegic home who had mastered the art of sketching and drawing by holding a pen in their mouths. When MP heard of them, he was bemused and at the same time motivated. One of them was Sergeant Rathore from the air force, a PT instructor who had suffered a spinal injury in an accident. He was so good at his art that the demand for his sketches was growing.

In the weeks that followed, a small board on a stand was procured, the height adjusted to be just in line with Anil's mouth. A paper was clipped to the board and MP was asked to hold a sketch pen in his mouth and write. In his own words, 'All my efforts to rationalise personal catastrophes have mystified and at times stupefied me. To adapt to the new challenges posed by the debility, I had to unshackle myself from the self-imposed stupor. Therefore, in September '90, I decided to learn the art of writing by holding a pen in my mouth. I began by scribbling illegibly, and was chagrined to find little progress after three weeks of laborious effort'.

He continues, 'Then I decided to change tactic and wrote a letter to Josie, the person who kept chivvying me to start mouth-writing. My joy knew no bounds when I completed the few lines that embodied my first mouth-written letter. Initially, I found my hard work to be a mere pie in the sky; but four to five months' assiduous efforts resulted in a readable style of writing'. He adds, 'This modest achievement enabled me to revive a chain of correspondence and beget new friends', and ends, 'it was a wonderful feeling to put down one's thoughts on paper'. A few months later, MP tried a sketch of Sarah—a side pose which brought out her features beautifully. This was promptly framed and adorned the wall near his bed.

In an interview in 1993 to a local newspaper, MP said, 'I looked upon writing as a way out of the stupor the accident had left me in. It was to reaffirm my faith in myself that I decided to learn to write holding a pen in my mouth'. This achievement gave Anil a second wind. Life was so much more meaningful now.

It wasn't easy. Holding the pen in his mouth for long periods made his jaws ache. Chewing on it to control it led to excessive salivation. ('Because the brain thought that I was eating something', MP explains.) His mouth would turn very dry subsequently, forcing him to drink water. To drink, MP had a glass bottle with a watertight top through which passed two tubes. One was for sucking the water while the smaller one was to equalise the low pressure created in the bottle.

A soft clean cloth was strapped to the pen to absorb the saliva and enable a good grip with less pressure of the jaw. MP's neck would ache due to the constant movement of the neck while writing. His eyes would water since the pen was held so close to the paper and his eyes had to squint at the letters at that short distance. Despite all this, he found writing an enjoyable and satisfying experience.

When he was tired or laid up in bed or not feeling too bright, MP would ask someone sitting around to write a letter for him. He dictated just as he would write, every comma in place. These letters were basically to his parents and sister at home, his friends in his squadron and close friends from school and NDA.

MP now began thinking about what he was to do with his life. Where will I settle after this hospitalisation phase is over? Who will look after my daily needs and help me in my daily chores? What has the air force planned for my future? Should I head to Chirayinkeezhu and stay at home? What are the special infrastructural requirements to settle at home? How would I get hospital care at home? What would my mobility be? Will my family be able to cope?

Many more questions needed to be answered. He discussed them with Sarah and she came up with several options and suggestions. Anil realised that his ageing parents would be overburdened if he went home. He would also cause a lot of mental agony to his family and he would have trouble finding timely hospital care. The nearest military hospital was in Trivandrum, 35 km away. Going back to his village was ruled out.

He then considered renting a room near the Kirkee hospital. Where would he find a 24X7 attendant? After 18-odd months in hospital, it would be very difficult to live by himself in a small hired room, he thought. He would be isolated. Sarah offered to shift in with him.

Another option available was to shift into the paraplegic home right next door. Here he would be amongst others like himself, get medical care as and when needed, and have all his administrative needs looked after.

But there was a problem. The paraplegic home was not established for 'officers'; only non-commissioned personnel were inmates. Also, the paraplegic home was almost full and MP would require a separate room to cater to his special needs. The more MP thought about it the more he was convinced that this suited him best.

Jacob Tharakan had a role to play in getting Anil into the paraplegic home. He had arrived in Pune on posting in 1990 and heard about his schoolmate admitted in the surgical ward.

'I didn't know where to start and asked the most stupid question to Anil—How are you?' he writes. Anil's response was clear and unambiguous, 'I am fine. Just want to get out of here!' Over the next few meetings, they chalked out a plan. Jacob wrote an application to the paraplegic home on MP's behalf. The application was accepted, but got stuck at the level of the GOC (General Officer Commanding) of the Sub Area in Pune. Luckily, Jacob was posted as ADC to the Commander of the Southern Army Command at Pune and he could give the necessary push to the application. He ensured that a letter was written by the Commander himself, allowing Anil to be the first 'officer' inmate at the home. This done, he writes, 'Operation "Getting Out" was successful and I was a relieved man'.

In the meantime, the medical board had decreed that Anil was no longer fit for service and would have to be 'boarded out' on medical grounds. It was the moral responsibility of the IAF to rehabilitate Anil in whatever way they could. MP was asked to take a decision about where he wanted to live after his release from service.

MP insisted on admission to the paraplegic home. He spoke to Sarah and managed to convince her that this decision was best for both of them. It was a decision from the head, though the heart tried its best to leverage the situation otherwise.

A beautifully written letter by MP lies in some corner of the hard disk of his computer today, along with some of his unpublished articles, in which he opens his heart to Sarah. Some of his friends, who were privy to that correspondence, say that he tried to make her see the practical side of things. If they decided to live together, he explained, Sarah would end up burdened for the rest of her life. Sarah needed to get on with her life too, have a family of her own and not get embroiled in a relationship that would bring her much grief. He said that though he would always remain indebted to her for all that she had done for him, the pillar of support she had been when he needed it most, the time had come to be more pragmatic and real.

The paraplegic home was being run under the aegis of the army formation in Pune, although it was a non-governmental, non-profit organisation run for the welfare of troops. The

CAS and the C-in-C of South Western Air Command got in touch with their army counterparts in Pune and after a number of meetings and discussions MP was permitted entry to the paraplegic home post 'retirement'. His mate from the home, Sunil Panicker adds, 'The final push to get admission came from the then Air Officer Commanding of Pune, Air Commodore Krishnaswamy. It was he who managed to convince the army. It was unprecedented for an officer to be admitted to the home'.

The home was full to capacity and the best that could be done was to shift MP into a room with two more inmates. Additionally, he was to be given a small workplace as his study. It was not possible at the time to give this special inmate a separate room, explains Sunil, but the study was a bonus and would take care of his intellectual needs.

It was almost two years after the accident. The rules allow two years of hospitalisation to any person for treatment and recovery whilst in active service. After this, depending on the utility of the person, a board of doctors decides on the degree of disability of the individual and whether he is fit for continuance in service. Based on this rule, and the fact that MP was almost 100 per cent disabled, it was decided to 'board out' MP. The orders were issued, and on April 12, 1990, Flying Officer Anil Kumar MP was discharged from service. He could use this rank as a prefix to his name for the rest of his life with the suffix 'Retired'. He was to get an enhanced 'disability' pension which would be sufficient to look after dependent family as well as his personal needs. A large number of senior officers of the air force had to amend and circumvent the rules to get the necessary government approvals for the enhanced disability pension.

During the period in hospital, it appears that there was not much contact with friends from school or NDA. I was fortunate to meet him every time I went to Pune on leave. Another close friend G Prakash, along with some course-mates who visited Pune on official tours, made it a point to visit the hospital. Sheeja also mentions a Malayali girl named Shobhana who worked and lived quite close to the hospital in Kirkee. She spent many a weekend at the hospital looking after MP in the initial days. Joy, MP's cousin, remembers that he stayed at Shobhana's place during his visits and she would cook Malayali food for MP and send it across to him on numerous occasions. My efforts at locating the lady remained unsuccessful despite a lot of efforts.

A course-mate, Bijoy Dhoj Rai, was also admitted in hospital around the time Anil arrived at Kirkee. He had suffered multiple bullet injuries during an operation against the LTTE in Sri Lanka and was recuperating at the hospital. Beedee, as he was known, was also in the ICU, barely able to walk after multiple surgeries to remove shrapnel from his body. He remembers meeting up with MP during his 'dark' days and often spent time by his bedside giving him mental and moral support. Beedee recuperated well, and went back into the fighting arms and became a brigadier. Last known, he was doing a stint as Military Attaché in France.

Vikram, his friend from Tezpur days, was posted in Pune when MP first arrived as a 'casualty' in 1988. He had lost touch with MP after the training in Tezpur but had followed his progress in the squadron at Pathankot. When he learnt that the casualty was his long-lost friend MP, he had been on the tarmac to receive him along with another of MP's batchmates, ARS Mendonca.

Later, they were the ones who searched the internet to get MP literature on paralysis and paraplegia. He writes, 'While we scoured the internet for a solution to the problem, it became increasingly clear that there was no cure available in modern medicine for him; MP was disappointed. But on meeting him, one could not discern any reduction in his cheerfulness and optimism—he retained an upbeat and cheerful demeanour. Here was a man so full of life that he refused to let go, moving on to find solutions for doing the things he wanted to despite his loss of normal ability'. It was this spirit, says Vikram, that made MP a favourite of all the nursing staff and doctors at the hospital. 'While being bedridden himself, he took a keen interest in the lives of those around him.' He adds, 'Not a year went by without the mouth-written season's greeting card arriving from him'.

In a mail to me, Vikram summarised MP's life for me in his own words: 'MP did not live a very long life, but the life he lived was lived fully. He epitomised the spirit of the IAF which is to never give up, to strive to achieve despite all the odds.' Eleven years ago, Vikram also suffered a nervous system injury which shortened his career as a fighter pilot. He writes, 'In the difficult times I have faced since then, MP has remained my guiding light. Whenever I feel myself losing hope or the will to fight, thinking about my association with MP puts iron back in my spine and gives me the motivation to fight on'.

Afterburners on, revving up

THE PARAPLEGIC Rehabilitation Centre (PRC) is located near the scenic and green Pune University campus. The idea of building this home for spinal injury personnel of the services was conceived after the Indo-Pak war of 1971. This war saw about 60 of our gallant soldiers suffering spinal cord injuries.

Such centres already existed in the USA (Veterans Home) and the UK (Spinal Cord Injury Centre, Aylesbury) besides some other European countries. The then Chief of Army Staff, General GG Bewoor, laid the foundation stone on June 23, 1973 and the centre was formally inaugurated by the President of India, Fakhruddin Ali Ahmed, on September 20, 1974.

Initially built for 24 casualties, the home was full by 1979 and there was a need to expand the capacity. By 1988, the centre had grown to 57 beds and four married quarters were also added to cater to the married paraplegics. By 1990 the home was again full, leading to a further increase in capacity to 83 single beds and 26 married quarters. This made the facility the largest of its kind in India and one of the largest in southeast Asia. Facilities and amenities like swimming pools, badminton courts, race tracks and therapy rooms have been added over time, making it an ideal rehabilitation home for people with spinal disability.

The centre is run by an ex-services doctor and a large number of specialised staff. Besides one administrative officer, there are nursing assistants, physiotherapists, a large number of attendants and support staff. They work tirelessly to look after the paraplegics and quadriplegics, helping them develop a positive outlook towards life, focusing on their ability rather than their disability. A large number of therapists and doctors visit the home regularly on a voluntary basis to provide free service to the inmates and the military hospital at Kirkee also chips in.

Funding for the home comes largely from the Armed Forces, but over the years a number of individuals and private and public organisations have also contributed to its coffers.

Most of the inmates here are given training at the Queen Mary Technical Institute (QMTI), located right next door in a sprawling 17-acre campus. The QMTI was founded by Lady Marie Willingdon, wife of the then Governor of Bombay Province, on May 16, 1917 in Bombay. The institute was shifted in 1922 to its present location.

The institute trains disabled armed forces personnel in vocational trades. Its beneficiaries include ex-armed forces personnel rendered unfit for service for medical reasons as well as those still in service but under prolonged medical treatment for severe disability. Later, they are assisted in rehabilitation. Dependants of servicemen/ex-servicemen may also be admitted, but only if there are leftover vacancies.

QMTI is the only institute of its kind in our country today (qmtiindia.org). Wheelchair-bound inmates of the PRC are trained here in management, computer hardware and software, and technical skills. Short courses are also offered in soft skills, such as personality development. After successful completion of training, soldiers go through a year's work experience. But for people like MP who are quadriplegics, QMTI offers no vocational training.

Besides comfortable accommodation, the PRC also has a well-equipped cookhouse and mess, a medical attention room, library and computer lab. The entire complex is built keeping the special requirements of paraplegics in mind. The PRC has been a pioneer in introducing sports on wheelchairs. They have a basketball court, a throwball court, racing track, swimming pool for hydrotherapy and a multi-purpose indoor sports complex.

The First National Games for the Disabled were organised by this institution and its residents have been undisputed champions in wheelchair sports at the national and international level, winning many awards. They have competed in paraplegic archery at championships held in China, Bangkok and South Korea. Six of the inmates have been selected to the national wheelchair basketball team. There are keen shuttle players too who have won championships at the national level and represented India in Indonesia, England and Spain.

MP was unable to use any of the sports facilities although he did venture out to the hydrotherapy pool occasionally. But being a sports enthusiast, he would often watch these keenly contested matches.

The squadron at Pathankot arranged for all MP's belongings to be delivered to his new home in Pune. His motorcycle was sold off in Pathankot and the money deposited in his account. MP realised that most of his clothes including his uniforms and shoes wouldn't be of any use anymore and decided to get rid of all the unnecessary stuff. All that he could wear now were loose shirts which had to be modified to open from the side and a lungi which could be draped around his lower half.

THE PARAPLEGIC home was much quieter than the hospital as there were fewer doctors, nurses and visitors milling around. MP felt a bit lost in his new environment. He also had to get accustomed to sharing his room with two colleagues who were quite hesitant to come forward and talk to the officer in their room. It would take him a few days to adapt to his new home. His brother and some cousins from home were around for company and made sure that he was comfortable. The books were arranged in the small study, his curios on the windowsills and on the bedside table. Posters and photographs went on to the walls and the room looked almost as good as it did in Pathankot. The TV was strategically placed so that MP could watch his favourite programmes from the bed.

The other two inmates in the room were soldiers from the northeast who had been injured in the militancy there. Both had excelled in table tennis and badminton. Many years down the line, on one of my usual visits to MP, I saw that one of the beds was empty and enquired about his whereabouts. MP cocked his head and looked heavenwards. Another year or so later, the other roommate also found a room to move into and MP joked, 'Two down, one to go!'

All the inmates were initially uncomfortable about having an 'officer' amongst them. They feared that MP would hog the limelight and boss them around, intruding on their privacy and freedom. But in time, they realised that the man was an inspiration and could do a lot to improve life at the home. MP soon became the leader of the inmates at his newfound home.

The first thing MP did was select a couple of attendants for himself. Since he was the only quadriplegic at the home, it was decided that MP would have one orderly round the clock, and therefore a set of four attendants were chosen to look after him. They were to operate in eight-hour shifts.

MP proposed that the attendants also look after other inmates. His instructions to them were to come and see him every half-hour during the time he was awake and turn him in bed three times during the night. One of his orderlies remembers what he told them, 'In case there is an emergency, I will cough loudly a number of times which will mean that I need help, so please keep your ears open as you do your duty'. He practised this 'emergency drill' a couple of times with them.

Over the years, some of these attendants changed jobs or retired. I met up with Arvind Baghade, Popat Shinde and Vinod Jagtap who looked after MP for many years with heart and soul. They have their own little stories and memories of MP to narrate. No wonder then that MP left part of his savings to these three men in appreciation for their services.

The attendants were expected to do almost everything 'except think', as MP put it to me once. It was like having an infant to look after. Jagtap gave me a vivid description of a typical 'MP day' at the paraplegic home when I met him whilst researching this book: 'I have been working at the PRC from 1997 and was working for Anil Saab right since then. Saab was a stickler for time. If I was even five minutes late with the food or to turn him around, I would get the firing of my life!'

Often MP would make Jagtap sit beside him and explain the importance of being on time and many other aspects of life. When MP was not well or in discomfort, he never showed it. He would stay calm and suffer silently, Jagtap remembers. Once when MP's favourite attendant Harbans Singh didn't turn up for work for a number of days, MP was worried. When Singh returned, MP asked him why he had been missing from duty without any information. Harbans explained that he had been blessed with a son after many years of marriage and had been busy with the celebrations. MP congratulated him and gave him some money. A few days later he was to learn that Harbans had been lying. 'He remained disturbed for the next few days', recalls Jagtap, 'and refused to have Harbans as his aide ever again'.

Food had to be served right on time. The attendant was expected to go to the kitchen beforehand and find out what was cooking. 'If it was karela (bitter gourd), tondli (ivy gourd), methi (fenugreek greens) or baingan (brinjal), we were not even supposed to mention it to him!' MP would avoid these vegetables in any form, he remembers. When the menu for the meal was spelt out, he would ask for a spoonful of each item to taste so that he could decide whether he was going to eat it. Once he knew what he wanted, a measured quantity would be brought from the kitchen. 'He would eat only one chapati and about six to seven small spoonfuls of rice', remembers his attendant.

MP had no way of telling when the stomach was full since the nerve connections from the stomach to the brain were not available. So only measured quantities could be eaten, else he would land up with a troubled stomach. 'This could be a major problem for the attendants as well as Saab', remembers Jagtap.

Mendonca or Mandy as he is called, a course-mate, remembers a time when he invited MP home for a day. Logistical arrangements were made well in advance and the trip finally materialised over a weekend. It was a south Indian menu which MP was fond of. Mandy decided to do away with the attendant and fed MP himself. MP loved the idlis and sambaar and Mandy kept insisting that MP eat a little more. MP landed up with an upset stomach, remembers Mandy.

When he was not happy with the menu, MP would ask the attendant to run down to a Kerala restaurant near the Kirkee bazaar and order some spicy chicken or fried fish or other south Indian food. He would still eat in small quantities. MP told me that he would often wait for the weekends when some of his friends would drop in, bringing some homemade food.

Anil once told Anniey, Jacob's wife, that he wanted to eat appams (pancakes made with fermented rice batter and coconut milk) with stew, a typical Malayali combination. By the time the dish reached Anil on the scooter, some of the stew had spilled. As he stood feeding Anil what was left in the tiffin, Jacob invited Anil to come home to eat the next time. On a prearranged Sunday, Jacob picked MP up, along with his wheelchair and attendant, for a day at home with the family. 'The trips had to be discontinued since MP couldn't move his chair to our loo and couldn't rest on our beds either', he writes.

Havildar Nadar is an ex-army soldier and former occupant of the home. Still wheelchair-bound, he lives quite close to the PRC with his wife and children. Since his wife belongs to the same village as MP, she took special care of MP's culinary requirements. In fact, MP's mother preferred to stay with the Nadar household over the years due to their genuine warmth and the proximity of their home to the PRC. MP loved the fried fish, idiappam, dosa and idli that Mrs Nadar made. As a token of his appreciation for the family, MP left a large sum of money in his will to them, but the Nadar family decided to gift it to the PRC.

A typical day for MP went something like this:

The early morning shift for the orderlies finished at 0530. Just before the orderly for the night shift left, he turned MP into a new position. A cup of tea arrived at 0600 and the new orderly propped him up and helped him sip it from the cup. The TV would then be put on with a Malayalam news channel feeding him the latest news in his mother tongue, keeping him informed of happenings closer home. While MP sipped his tea, he would flick to some sports channels. Before he moved in for his ablutions, MP would ask his attendant to show him the newspaper page by page. He would go over the headlines and make a mental note of what was to be read in detail later.

On one of his visits to the home, Jacob Tharakan saw that MP shooed away his attendant when Jacob entered. He learnt that the attendant had been reading the day's newspaper to MP in his rather limited English. This led to Operation Reading Board.

A newspaper stand was fabricated by the carpenters in Jacob's unit. An engineer helped add adjustable bands and angle-holds.

Tea was followed by a frugal breakfast and then it was time for the loo. Another attendant came down to help transfer MP to the special wheelchair used for the ablutions. This wheelchair had two air-filled scooter tubes, one to sit on and the other as a backrest. In the washroom, MP would supervise the brushing of his teeth sitting in his wheelchair in front of the mirror. 'It had to be done in a particular manner', remembers Jagtap. The attendant would then give him a shave and move the wheelchair over the Indian-style commode. 'We had to apply some pressure in his groin area for the evacuation to happen', says Jagtap. After this it was time for him to be wheeled into the bathing area. Bath over and body dried, his hair would be oiled and brushed in the typical MP style and his body powdered and checked for any signs of bedsores. A loose shirt was slipped over him and he was made to sit on the lungi which was spread over the seat of the chair. This was then draped over his lower torso. MP, now fresh and clean and dressed for the day, would be shifted into the normal wheelchair and wheeled into the study where he would spend time studying in the initial years and later, on the computer when he got one.

MP put in three hours-plus on the computer on a good morning. This was punctuated with a tea break when a cup of black tea without sugar was savoured before getting back to work. If someone came visiting, MP would notice them passing by the window on his left through the corner of his eye. His eyes would light up and his face would break into a smile; he would do a quick save and exit, dropping the long pencil into his lap.

Then, depending on the weather and the mood, he would ask to be wheeled into the corridor or ask for a chair to be placed for the visitor, his own chair adjusted to have the person sitting right in front of his keen eyes. A long conversation would thus begin.

By 1245, MP would be wheeled out of his room into the living area and propped into his bed. Lunch would arrive by 1300, and take no more than 10 minutes to finish. He would then sip water and be turned on his side. Here, a newspaper opened to the page he wanted awaited on a stand at the edge of his bed. He often fell asleep reading, remember his orderlies. But by the end of the evening, between naps, he would have read the newspaper from cover to cover.

A cup of tea arrived for MP around 1630 after which he was wheeled out into the corridor to watch the day turn to night. Sitting here, he greeted fellow inmates at their evening 'walks' or watched them playing in the courts nearby. The bougainvillea flowering outside would mark the passage of time and the seasons. He could also clearly see aircraft flying over the Lohegaon air base and he would watch with a bitter-sweet nostalgia. Sometimes, if the weather was inclement or he had some pending work to do, he would ask to be taken to the computer where he sat till dinner was announced or he felt tired. If the dinner menu was not to his liking, an orderly would be quietly dispatched to get some vegetable biryani and chicken, remembers his orderly.

Post-dinner he was helped into his bed and propped up a bit so he could watch his favourite channels, watch the news and then read the paper sleeping on his side. He often fell asleep around 1030 while reading, remembers his attendant. 'Anil Saab was interested in watching football. Every weekend, when there was a live match, he would watch it late into the night until it ended. No match of the World Cup was missed.' Brazil was his favourite team.

Computing

IT WAS Group Captain PI Murlidharan or Murli who, in 1992, suggested that MP get himself a personal computer. But how was it to be operated? Several ideas were mooted and set aside. MP would require a keyboard modified to his requirements and would have to learn to operate the software efficiently. The Air Force Wives Welfare Association (AFWWA) at the Pune air force base decided to present MP his first computer—a basic 286 machine.

I requested my father-in-law, Wing Commander RV Jog, a technical officer who had retired from the air force in 1985, to meet MP and understand his specific requirements. Wing Commander Jog and his friend Dr A Kulkarni explored the market for a suitable machine. The most important part of the equipment, they realised, would be a specially designed keyboard. Till such time a machine was procured, the duo suggested that MP learn programming. MP readily agreed.

They found MP a very bright student, ever ready to absorb what they threw at him. 'He would ask a lot of questions, all based on logic', mused my father-in-law. It was logic that ran the computer and it was easy for MP to pick up some basic and higher languages. MP's interest was fired, and he bought some books for self-study.

Computer books were expensive in those days. While Jog and Kulkarni got him a few which they had used themselves, MP decided to send his cousins in search of books on C, C++, FoxPro, Visual Basic and later HTML and Java scripting. The street-side vendors in Pune offered some second-hand books at reduced prices. Soon a large number of these books adorned the bookshelves in his room and MP spent a lot of time understanding the nuances of computing.

Another of MP's fans and fellow inmates at the home was Sunil Panicker. An Indian Navy diver, he had suffered a diving accident and came to the home soon after MP did. He told me, 'One of MP's friends was a Colonel in the army. His father, a spiritual leader of sorts, came to visit MP once. So impressed was the father with MP that he presented him 12 volumes of the entire works of Swami Vivekananda'. 'Within no time MP had read these and could quote from them during discussions. He also read the works of Sri Aurobindo', Sunil remembers.

After a few months of in-depth study, MP was good enough to start teaching programming language, says Kulkarni. My father-in-law, who was on the governing body of the QMTI, suggested that MP go to the institute and try his hand at teaching programming and some soft skills to the students there. This was not feasible for MP and the idea was binned. The computer gifted by AFWWA was upgraded in 1995 to a 386.

I also remember how we course-mates helped him upgrade the machine in 2004, the 20th year of our service. I wrote to each person in our batch while I was posted in Patiala, reminding them that we needed to remember those who had left us and do something for those who required our help, especially MP who had been one of us through our journey in the IAF. Replies and funds poured in and we could buy him the latest machine available in the market in those times. If I had told MP what we were doing, I am sure he would have asked us to donate the money to someone more needy.

But every time a machine was changed, MP had to go through the painful rigmarole of setting it up the way he wanted it.

I was lucky to get in touch with an Indian family in the US who had a quadriplegic child who had recently passed away, aged 18. They wanted to gift the special equipment used by the child to a deserving paraplegic. They also suggested we get a page-turner and a curved keyboard for MP. The curved keyboard would ensure that the keys placed in a semicircle could be accessed more easily, without much movement of his neck, reducing the strain. The page-turner of course would help MP read as and when he wished, without an orderly standing by to turn the pages. It just required a word command or a blink of an eye to turn the page, they explained.

Sarah continued her visits to MP and encouraged MP in his quest for computer knowledge. She ensured that MP continued to practise his mouth-writing. It was slow and laborious and she kept at MP to continue. By 1992, MP had started sending 'signed' cards to friends and relatives and all of us who were privileged to receive them. I received an anniversary card every year after '92, and it was the best gift anyone ever gave me.

Jacob Tharakan also had a role to play in Anil's mouth-writing. He arranged for the stationery and the sketch pens that were best suited to be held in the mouth. He writes, 'The exercise was a little frustrating in the beginning and the progress slow. However, in about two months, Anil had managed to write quite a lot and I requested him for one mouth-written page as a trophy'. Anil refused, saying that he needed to get better at it. A few weeks later, MP asked him to open his cupboard and pick up a signed page that he had specially written for him. 'It remains the best gift that I ever got from anyone', Jacob writes. 'More than him achieving something, I felt that I had conquered the world.' Ramesh Menon of *India Today* did a story on the paraplegic home around the time MP was grappling with the computer procurement. 'Prashant Panjiar, the photographer with the team, offered to get me a trolley to suit my requirements', writes MP. Panjiar got MP to speak to his friend Arun Jethmalani in Delhi who dealt in computer furniture. MP also spoke to Iftekhar Sayed, Arun's friend in Pune, who was designing the keyboard for his computer and made sure the two met and coordinated the overall requirements.

A trolley with many swinging or rotating arms and a heavy base was designed, much like the one we see in hospitals. One of the 'arms' would hold the keyboard vertically, the other held the monitor on a pedestal, while still another had a writing pad with clips to allow MP to read from any material he required. The keyboard height was adjusted to his mouth level, while the pad was positioned to the right and above and the monitor screen just left of it and behind. It was an ingenious arrangement which worked well for MP (see picture).

Sayed managed to fix a mouse in an inverted position on the keyboard so that the track ball could be moved around with a stick held in the mouth. Besides that, he also designed a number of shortcut keys which did away with the need to double-click the mouse or use two keys simultaneously. This innovation was essential for MP to use the machine independently. He also designed a stick which would help MP peck at the keys without much movement of the neck. A long pencil with the little plastic hand at one end that we used as children was chosen. The plastic end of the fingers of this 'hand' were chiselled a bit and the wooden end thickened for better grip. This done, MP could hold the pencil over the thickened portion and manipulate the plastic end inside the mouth to manage a pecking motion with ease. It was an ingenious invention which enabled the next turning point—life with the computer as his best friend.

'Saab's life did another U-turn with the arrival of the computer in the room', remembers his orderly. There was a visible new sprightliness and purpose. He wanted to be up and about early and spend as much time on the machine as possible, reading and working. He also managed to connect to the internet. Getting a stable connection wasn't easy in those times. Some pressure on the telephone department by his friends in the army helped expedite the process.

Using the computer for long durations had its own problems. It caused eyestrain, neck pain, and aching jaws. This was no deterrent for the committed man who soldiered on. A yoga teacher visiting the paraplegic home taught him some exercises to reduce the discomfort. He continued with them throughout his life till the very end, and it paid him rich dividends.

In 1991, on his 27th birthday, Anil received another beautiful gift from the air force. It was a sophisticated, battery-operated, motorised wheelchair made in Canada. A chin-operated joystick controlled the motion of the chair and it was also fitted with the latest safety features.

Murli had a major role to play in its procurement. He got in touch with a quadriplegic British policeman through his brother Suvarthan who was in England at the time. Suvarthan was directed to the Canadian company which had provided the Englishman a wheelchair that could be controlled by his breath. The Canadian company was immediately told of MP's special requirement and a wheelchair with chin-operated controls was suggested. With a little push through diplomatic channels, the cost of the wheelchair was sponsored by the government. The Defence Attaché in the US arranged to transport it to India. Air India flew the chair to Pune free of cost.

And that was how MP became a 'chairborne' warrior. Soon he was moving about independently within the premises. Writing to thank Murli for his efforts in enabling this mobility, in his inimitable style, MP writes, 'The chair is very sophisticated, the only thing it lacks is an "afterburner!"' Later, he joked to me that he could now whizz around at 8 kmph as against the 800 kmph in his MiG-21.

The chair served MP well for a few years, but started giving trouble around 1995. There was an electrical glitch that made it stop and start with a jerk, not a good thing for MP's neck.

The batteries were also giving up with age and a new set was not available in the country. The aircraft technicians at the Air Force Station tried their best to get it back on line but were unsuccessful. The company which manufactured the chair was contacted, but they had stopped manufacturing the product and had moved on to some other business. Sadly, the chair was covered up and relegated to one corner of his room. MP told me that he could not risk injury with the bad motor movement and it was best to use the manual one till such time as this one could be repaired.

Much later, during my posting to NDA, I took the wheelchair to a local mechanic friend who claimed that the only problem was a faulty chip in the circuit which needed to be changed. The electronic markets in Pune, Mumbai and Delhi were scoured by friends, but we were unsuccessful. The sophisticated chair was dead for good. MP had experienced a freedom of mobility that had enlivened his life for a few years; a freedom that he had cherished but lost.

In time he went on to learn web designing and did a wonderful job designing the web page of the PRC, linking it to many similar institutions and people worldwide. This helped the inmates interact with others like them, and to find out more about disability. 'This web page provided the basic platform for future upgradations. Though tweaked several times, the web page is still being used by the PRC today', says an inmate.

As he gained proficiency and experience in operating the machine, he literally took over the running of the computers at the PRC. As I sat chatting with him in the corridor one day, one of the inmates came huffing up on his wheelchair, telling him about a problem with one of the computers in the accounts department. He was petrified that the data would be lost.

MP was cool. 'Tell me the problem again?' Like a doctor analysing the symptoms of a patient, MP issued a clear set of instructions, and before long the inmate returned beaming from ear to ear, reporting success. All the inmates of the home were involved in administration in some way or the other. While one looked after the accounts, another functioned as the PRO, or managed the correspondence or helped in the cookhouse. It was a good arrangement since it gave the inmates something constructive to do and also helped the home run better. MP willy-nilly became chief of the computer department.

COLONEL SP JYOTI retired from the Army Medical Corps and took up employment at the paraplegic home in Kirkee. He had been posted at Kirkee when MP arrived from Pathankot in 1988, and had treated him during the hospital stay too. He stayed on as director of the PRC from 1990 until just a month before MP's death in 2014. Colonel RK Mukherjee took over from Jyoti and is currently in charge of the home. Dr Jyoti was able to fill me in on MP's last year at the home.

I often made it a point to visit Dr Jyoti at the home. Firstly, I would hear from him how MP was doing and if he was having any medical or personal problems. Secondly, I was able to give him feedback about the running of the home that MP was reluctant to give him directly.

During one visit to Dr Jyoti's home as part of my research, he asked me umpteen times, 'Why wasn't I told that he passed away? I looked after him for so many years and this was the least they could do... why didn't they inform me, I wonder?' Mukherjee explained that Jyoti was informed of the demise but he was too overwhelmed to come for the funeral. Perhaps he has forgotten details, but his eyes still light up when asked about MP.

MP had a sweet and sour relationship with the old man. He was a doctor par excellence, but when it came to administering the home, MP felt 'he was too decent for the job'. The home was strapped for funds at the time and some measures to remedy the tight financial situation were not appreciated by the inmates.

Since the electricity bills were very high, it was decided to charge all inmates extra for all the gadgets they owned. The inmates were asked to chip in for the air-conditioners, coolers, irons, chargers etc. The inmates felt the electricity bill was the sole responsibility of the management.

MP decided to confront Jyoti and tell him that this decision was too harsh on the ex-servicemen who often had to manage two or three establishments on their disability pension. He was, however, ready to pay the charges for the air-conditioner that he had himself installed. The matter remained unresolved and someone decided to write an anonymous letter to the Army Commander. The commander responded quickly, and the issue was resolved in favour of the inmates. Jyoti wasn't happy about the way it was done. 'I think he suspected that I wrote the letter', said a smiling MP to me one day.

Another issue that MP often complained about was the poor catering. It was important that the inmates be fed well and kept healthy, but there were some hygiene issues that MP was worried about. I conveyed this to Jyoti on one of my visits. Jyoti hinted at the paucity of funds. He felt MP was too finicky about his food.

Differences also simmered between the management and the permanent staff at the PRC regarding working conditions and emoluments. Matters came to a head in August 1995 and the attendants decided to go on strike when the chairman, Brigadier CJ Appachu, didn't accede to their demands.

The strike lasted about six weeks, remembers Sunil Panicker. But it got people like MP thinking. He shot off a letter to Justice Krishna Iyer (an old family friend from the Chirayinkeezhu days) seeking his opinion on the legality of the strike. He argued that the inmates had a right to life and their lives were dependent on the availability of the attendants. MP said that just as doctors were required to treat patients and save their lives, the attendants were the lifeline for the inmates. He went on to explain that this right to life was being violated by the striking workers and their service be brought under the Essential Services Maintenance Act. Justice Iyer went through the facts of the case and opined that the attendants, as per the law of the land, had a right to protest and strike work.

This irked MP. In an article on rediff.com in 1997, MP writes, 'While the arrival of the temporary army staff baulked the striking lot's intention of completely paralysing the functioning of the centre, the inmates had to put up with unspeakable hardships. By striking en masse, they had endangered not only our paralysed bodies but our lives too. One dreads to imagine what would have happened in a similar situation to the inmates of an institution with lesser resources'. He adds, 'Our mammoth statute book seems to be armed with all conceivable laws under the sun, yet, not surprisingly, there is no law banning strikes in such institutions'.

As an emergency measure, the army had pooled in resources from the Army Medical Corps and a local Maratha Light Infantry (MLI) unit so that the inmates could be looked after. Although they were taken care of by these soldiers, the case was analysed and talked about for a long time.

Around the same time as the strike, another incident shook up the inmates. There was pressure on Colonel Jyoti to identify inmates who were fit enough to be sent home for further management: there were many paraplegics waiting for admission to the home. Since the older lot were settled in life and had even found occupations, it was felt that they should give way to fresh inmates. The 'expulsion' soon began and before they knew it, almost 10 to 12 inmates were sent away to fend for themselves.

'In those days, a call to an inmate to appear before the director would send shivers down their spines', explains Panicker. There was palpable tension at the home, he remembers. Some of the inmates including himself contemplated committing suicide to protest and publicise this injustice nation-wide, he told me. 'It was impossible for me to even think of a life outside of the home, despite the fact that I had some amount of family support. I was convinced that they would not be able to look after my special requirements, and therefore, to die was a better option.'

MP was not a silent observer in all this. The inmates confided in him their fears and asked him to do something. MP was after all an 'officer', and that too well-connected, they said. He was totally against the evictions and he decided to intervene. He convinced a retired Brigadier, NB Grant, to write an article on the issue in the *Maharashtra Herald*. This started a debate in the letters to the editor column. It stalled the evictions temporarily, but no decision was taken in writing by the management to stop the same.

MP now decided to write to the Commander-in-Chief of the South Western Air Command, Air Marshal Krishnaswamy, who had done a lot for MP as the boss of the air base in Pune. 'Kicha' Sir was not a man who would keep silent in such a case and MP was confident that some action would be taken soon. A few weeks later, the staff and administration at the home were seen doing some rapid cleaning and painting on the campus. Someone big was coming. A large number of officers in greens came next, indicating that it was to be someone senior from the army.

It was to be General S Padmanabhan, then C-in-C of the South Western Army Command (who rose to be Chief of Army Staff). He inspected the campus with Jyoti and the chairman in tow. He met the inmates and, in the end, walked into MP's room. MP was seated at his computer and welcomed him with his charismatic smile. The General looked at MP and quipped, 'Kicha has told me everything, you need not worry, I am sorting out the issue', even as a bewildered Jyoti and the Brigadier looked on. The matter of eviction had been resolved. After this, MP became the unrivalled leader of the inmates of the home.

IN 1993, WHEN MP was just getting to know about computers and computing, he came across an announcement of an essay contest in *The Indian Express*'s Citizen magazine. Readers were invited to write about the 'turning point' in their lives in about 1,000 words. MP claimed that he coined the word 'chairborne' for this article, a word that was to become strongly associated with him. The article was aptly titled 'Airborne to Chairborne' and spoke about his battle against disability.

'I still wasn't writing on the computer', remembers MP, 'so I decided to send a mouth-written piece. My mouth-writing was not as well-formed then and the font was large, so my article ran into a large number of pages.' So impressed were the publishers with his article that they decided to publish it as it was written rather than typesetting it. It ran across six pages of the magazine and MP received the first prize of Rs 500. The article is reproduced in this book, just as he wrote it.

A lady professor in charge of revision of textbooks for the Secondary School Certificate (SSC) Board happened to read the article. She got MP's permission to include it in the English textbook being used by Class X students studying in Maharashtra State Board schools. Overnight, the man became a celebrity. Letters of appreciation began to pour in from different parts of the state and a large number of children became his fans. MP writes, 'Most of the letters are out of curiosity because I write with my mouth, but I reply to each one of them'.

Besides some teachers and students who were inspired to come and meet MP on their own, schools began to send their students to the home as part of their 'socially useful and productive work' class. Whilst they were there, they looked at MP in awe and asked him a million questions, which he was only too happy to answer. Suddenly, he was busy and famous. Some students and teachers began writing to him asking for advice on personal matters too. MP said to me, 'I am no expert on most of the issues that people want to confide in me. I try to answer all the queries I can, but direct them to specialists to find answers to questions I don't have a clue about'.

The same year, in 1993, Acchan, Anil's father, passed away at the age of 65. Anil went very quiet, not meeting anyone. Jyoti, fearing that MP would go into depression, decided to call Jacob whom he knew as MP's good friend. He did not tell Jacob why he was wanted immediately. 'My heart sank. I picked up my scooter and drove the 16-odd km to the home deep in thought', writes Jacob. He found a forlorn MP sitting in his chair. 'He didn't give me time to ask him anything. He asked me to hug him tight. As I did so, MP sobbed and his body went into spasms. For a few minutes that felt like ages, he continued to weep in my arms.' As he regained his composure, Anil broke the news to Jacob. 'I had never seen him cry before', Jacob says.

Soaring again

MP'S LIFE had come full circle. He had overcome the terrible tragedy and come out smiling, with few complaints. He had acquired the ability to observe calmly the tumult of the world, without judgement, standing apart from it, and yet participating fully in every aspect of life. Suvarthan, Murli's brother, describes it thus: 'With no limbs or body to talk about, all the energies seem to have been concentrated in his head... The body was delinking itself, the world was becoming more and more unapproachable by the senses, but the mind was still active, yearning to touch other lives, make a difference.'

MP had indeed started to make a perceptible impact on the lives of those who came in touch with him. Besides people like BD Rai, Vikram, Sarah and many others at the Paraplegic home, there were others too whose stories need to be told. MP, they claim, still lives with them in their hearts. Some of the stories are presented in this chapter. I was lucky to get the email addresses of all MP's contacts and wrote to them. I was also involved in forming an MP Anil Kumar Fan Club, along with Vishwanathan Girish, a friend on Facebook. The fan club has now grown in leaps and bounds. I received a large number of inputs from all MP's friends and I am indebted to them for sharing their experiences. I regret that I have not been able to include all the responses received.

People who came in touch with MP were intrigued to find him calm and cheerful. Most of those who met him the first time wondered how they would begin their conversation with him. MP surprised them all. He was always ready for visitors. The only thing that upset him a little was when people did not keep their appointments and landed up at odd hours when he was resting or having his meals. He always told me, 'You can come anytime, but I will be more comfortable to see others while I am on my chair; so the ideal time is between 0930 to 1230 and then in the evening at about 1700 to 1900 hours'. He liked to be dressed properly while he met new people and found it embarrassing when someone new landed up while he was lying bare-chested.

The second thing that continued to amaze people was the depth of his knowledge. From sports to politics to technology, he was able to discuss almost anything under the sun. And if he heard of something that he didn't know about, rest assured, the next time you met him, he would have studied the subject in detail. With his interest in varied subjects, he was able to write so many articles in different publications. He was able to keep his audience completely engaged, and to top it all there was his fantastic wit and humour.

One could sit with him for hours and not notice time fly.

I looked forward to my visits to MP at the paraplegic home. I miss them now. It was like entering a different world. From the hustle and bustle of the city, I would be transported to a serene and quiet atmosphere, with just a touch of the sombre. A number of soldiers would be moving about on wheelchairs, with or without the support of attendants, depending on the severity of their disability. They would be engaged in conversation over cups of tea or coffee being sold at the kiosk run by one of them in a corner of the home, adjoining the main road. I would find MP either sitting in the verandah chatting with some visitors or sitting at his computer in his small room, working feverishly, pecking at his keyboard. Sometimes, on Sundays, one found a horde of children along with their teachers sitting in a semi-circle around him absorbing every word that he said. The audience would once in a while erupt into peals of laughter hearing his witty answers to their numerous questions.

As he recognised you, the long pencil would drop into his lap and a welcoming smile would appear. The attendant would be called in to shut down the machine after the file was saved and we would begin our conversation, without a moment to waste. Later, the attendant would appear to tell us it was time for lunch or dinner... sometimes MP would wave him off with a gesture of his head and ask him to delay the meal by 10 minutes. It was very difficult to disengage from MP. You returned refreshed and recharged after each meeting. Only those who knew him will understand exactly how I felt.

FLIGHT CADET Herojit Rajkumar Singh, 'Hero' to his friends and family, belonged to a small village of Singjamei in Manipur, in the far-eastern corner of India. He joined the NDA as a pilot aspirant in the 119 Course and passed out as the Battalion Cadet Adjutant. He blazed through the academy, excelling in swimming and sports and bagging the coveted Best Cadet in Physical Training trophy before passing out and moving to the Air Force Academy.

At AFA, he stood third in the basic flying stage. He moved on to the Fighter Training Wing (FTW) at Hakimpet (Secunderabad) for the advanced level. During a solo sortie on August 22, 2011 he faced a grave emergency which forced him to eject at low level. The force of the ejection caused his lumbar spine to snap, although the parachute-assisted descent was safe. Hero followed the same route as MP to land up at the military hospital in Kirkee as a paraplegic who had lost the use of his lower limbs. Barely 20, he was told that he would be in a wheelchair all his life and to top it all, he was to be boarded out as a cadet without any pensionary benefits. The young boy was completely devastated and pleaded with the doctors, 'Sir, I know I can't be a pilot, but my upper body is okay, so can't I serve the IAF in a non-flying capacity?' 'You are not even commissioned as an officer, son, I am afraid you will have to be boarded out…There is no rule which permits you any further help from the government', he was told.

As his world came tumbling down, Hero began to look for other options. He began cramming for competitive exams and continued to knock on all doors to explain his case. During this time he met MP, who he had heard about as he lay recuperating, supine on his bed in hospital. MP listened to his story and felt deeply empathetic. Surely the IAF would be able to help, he thought to himself.

Hero wrote to me, 'I was one of the lucky people who got to spend a lot of time with Anil Sir. I used to make it a point to go to him every Wednesday at about 9 in the morning and spend a couple of hours with him to get as motivated as he was'. Anil told him that he was aware of the policy on boarding out of service. 'If the policy can be changed for the good of all, why can't we try?' he said. MP got Hero to write an application which was addressed through the formal channels to the Air Officer Commanding at Hakimpet. 'Anil Sir followed it up by writing letters to different people in the chain to ensure that my application moved in the right direction', writes Hero.

At about this time, the Air Force decided to award Anil a 'Commendation by the CAS' for services rendered and his 'never say die' attitude. This followed just after the Commander-in-Chief of the South Western Army Command had commended Anil for services rendered whilst at the paraplegic home. The Chief of Air Staff, Air Chief Marshal NAK Browne, was himself coming to the paraplegic home to pin the small silver medal on MP at an event organised at the PRC.

MP saw this as an opportunity to get young Hero to meet the CAS face to face. He briefed the staff at Air HQ on what he had planned so that the CAS could be briefed in advance. The CAS came over to Anil's room on that day in July 2012 and the formality of pinning the medal to Anil's shirtsleeve was completed. After the journalists and photographers had had their photo op and receded, MP opened up the topic of Hero with the chief. Hero was also present in the room and writes, 'Anil Sir was so selfless; it was his day but most of the time was spent talking about my case with the CAS'. He tried to convince the boss that a paraplegic could be productive working from his wheelchair and cited examples of paraplegic officers who were already in service. Finally the CAS said to Hero, 'I cannot give you an assurance as of now as the decision has to be taken at the level of the Defence Minister, but I promise to give it a good shot'.

In fact, when I met him just a few days after the visit of the CAS, MP told me in jest, 'I spoke so much about Hero that I think I managed to bug the boss!' In an article written in rediff.com in June 2013, Anil writes, 'With the chief's assurance, Hero's hopes took wing but he refrained from exulting as he was aware that there were a whole lot of hurdles that needed to be crossed in the bureaucracy'. He continues, 'His file began the customary back-and-forth between the MoD and Air HQ, the latter having to respond to the clarifications sought by the former. It redounds to the credit of the CAS that he bypassed the normally nay-saying bureaucrats by reasoning with the Defence Minister directly'. Anil also asked Hero to get some political pressure applied through his family and the member of parliament from Manipur, who promised to meet the Defence Minister in person. In addition, copies of Hero's bio-data were sent to the Chief Minister of Manipur who did some rallying from that end too. In the third week of December, with the pulls and pressures from all quarters, the Defence Minister finally signed and stamped the imprimatur of Hero's retention.

The IAF and Flying Officer Herojit Rajkumar Singh made history. Hero is perhaps the first wheelchair-bound cadet to be commissioned by any of the armed forces in the world. Today,

Hero works as an accounts officer at one of the operational bases of the IAF and is doing extremely well. An important aspect of the article written in *rediff,* 'The flight cadet who never gave up', about Hero is that MP does not once mention his own involvement in the affair!

ALL THROUGH his stay at the paraplegic home, MP was in touch with his friends from Sainik School. He was concerned about the way all Sainik Schools, his school in particular, were being administered. MP wrote an article which snowballed into a movement to revive the Sainik Schools in 2008.

Over time, and for a number of reasons, the Sainik Schools have failed to become the feeder institutes or nurseries of military officers. In his article titled 'Tokenism won't revive Sainik Schools' published in 2008 in *rediff.com*, MP explores the main reasons for the failure of these institution. 'The Sainik Schools—the brainchildren of the late Defence Minister VK Krishna Menon—were midwived under the aegis of the Sainik School Society (SSS) in 1961 as a hybrid institution managed by both the centre and the States... It was thus congenitally tailor-made for passing the buck'. The States were to provide the land, infrastructure, maintenance and scholarship, but these obligations were not formalised, leaving loopholes. MP goes on to explain that the entire budget provided by the central defence budget for the schools is utilised for the salaries and pensions of the serving and ex-serving staff, leaving nothing for development of infrastructure and the students—unarguably the two most important ingredients of any institution. The State government is, therefore, forced to recover the growing costs from the parents.

'The Supreme Court in 1989 directed the SSS to extend pension and gratuity to all employees. The SSS didn't have the means, the States looked the other way, forcing the parents to cough up', writes MP in the article. The Sainik Schools had become nobody's baby—superintended by the defence ministry, hosted by the States and bankrolled by the parents! 'Ever heard of parents footing the salary and pension of the staff of a government-owned school? Absurd, right? No wonder the bill per student of Rs 11,000 in 1989 zoomed to Rs 55,000 this year', MP wrote.

With the Sixth Pay Commission around the corner, the bills were headed skywards, setting off alarm bells that no one wanted to hear at the time. Background parleys began with a series of mails between MP and Colonel 'Ike' Isenhower, a 1972 batch pass out of the same school. Ike was at the time serving in the Intelligence Bureau and sat in North Block, well-connected with the bureaucracy. He writes, 'Sitting in North Block, I had a coercive power handle, probably better than many, to connect with the crazy bureaucracy. The passion for the school was our common chord; we often complemented each other; often pulled and heaved together'.

Ike says he requested Sandeep Unnithan of *India Today* to highlight the plight of the school cadets. A translated article soon appeared in *Punjab Kesari* which finally ended up being discussed in parliament, thanks to some pushing by another upcoming journalist, another ex-student from the 1991 batch, Josy Joseph.

Two things happened as a result. First, the post of the SSS head, a serving Colonel, was upgraded to a Brigadier who, it was expected, would use his star rank to push the cause of the

Sainik Schools. Second, the Defence Minister was compelled to have a closer look at the problem and he doled out Rs 2 crore to each Sainik School to cover the deficit.

Commenting on the financial help provided by the government, MP writes, 'Though beneficial in a way, the Rs 44-crore pledge will ultimately end like water off a duck's back; it will neither unburden the fee-paying parents nor induce certitude amongst the staff'. He goes on to add, 'If the finance minister picked up the annual tab of all 22 schools, he knew it would be incurring a burden to the tune of Rs 80-85 crore to the exchequer. So, instead of grasping the bull by its horns, I suspect the politician in him emerged to the fore and opted for the easy way out, earmarking a one-time subsidy. But he surely knows that national security doesn't come cheap. *A nation neglects its security at its peril.* And Sainik Schools are a pivotal cog in the security apparatus'.

In the end, MP summarises, 'It is the lack of access to Sainik Schools for the son of Everyman, the probable officer aspirant, owing to the sky-high fees that has precipitated the intake shortage. Inferior infrastructure is incidental to the crisis. If the defence ministry wasn't myopic and had responded in 1989 itself by embracing the salary and pension obligation, the present pickle could have been avoided. Its chronic inaction has almost lain waste what it begat in 1961. The ministry has an opportunity now to make amends for its historic blunder—take over all 22 Sainik Schools. Since the issue is organically linked to national security, one expects another dollop of munificence from the Finance Minister, and hopes that he and the Defence Minister shall join forces to cleave through the red tape to sanction the necessary budgetary allocation for all Sainik Schools'.

In the same article he suggests measures to resuscitate the Sainik Schools: To facilitate the rebirth of the Sainik Schools, the Sainik School Society needs to be dismantled hook, line and sinker. The centre needs to take charge of the situation and bring all these schools under the Integrated Defence Staff headquarters, much like the National Defence Academy, and bear its entire expenses. This expenditure will be worth it he says, 'as it will ensure perpetual supply to the academies, thus fulfilling the original aim of the venture'.

The man just couldn't be put down... he was forthright, focused and fearless in the pursuit of his goals.

THERE WERE many strangers who sought MP out for counsel and strength. Sangeeta was one of them. A doctor by profession, she served in the air force for five years till 2004 during which time she got married to a fighter pilot, who unfortunately died in an air crash just around the time she was leaving the IAF. She read about MP on the internet and wrote to him. Pat came the reply and soon she was headed to Pune to meet him. The chemistry was instant, they got talking about the air force, squadron life and their lives after the accidents. 'Everything in his room showed how deeply attached he was to the air force, there were aircraft posters everywhere. MP's photos with the aircraft he flew were on the walls and even the calendars and stationery were marked with the IAF symbol.'

They got into a long discussion about the meaning of life. In a mail to me, she writes, 'I realised the temporary and illusive nature of *maya*; how our life can be toppled in a few seconds and how one can be reduced to live in the most uncomfortable circumstances in the same time. I was bewildered at how someone could live a life of dignity in a situation such as MP's. It awakened in me the gratitude with which I should live my own life, a life I took for granted for so long and didn't appreciate. It also made me a more sensitive person, more so, as being a doctor, I saw so many patients in distress every day'. As she left the home that day, she promptly went to the office of Colonel Jyoti and handed him a donation, extracting a promise not to inform MP about the same.

Practising her profession in Dubai, Sangeeta did manage to keep track of MP's health through her doctor friends in Pune. She often advised him about the medicines to take when he was not keeping too well and the precautions that needed to be taken.

Sangeeta managed to reach MP's bedside just a few days before his demise. As she sat next to him, she whispered Shree Krishna's holy name in his ears as she held his twisted hands with tears streaming down her face. That was all she could do at that stage.

SAYALI SHINTRE is a doctor today. She first read about MP in his essay in her school English textbook. 'It was a lesson for a lifetime', she writes. She decided to write to MP and tell him how he had enabled her to see the positive side of life. The letter reached MP, but the little girl had forgotten to put her address at the back of the envelope. She knew she wouldn't receive a reply. But a few days later a letter did arrive, written in MP's neat 'hand'. First, MP pointed out her negligence and then went on to answer her questions. He had observed the name of her village on the top of the envelope and decided to ask another of his fans from the same village whether he could trace Sayali. This boy's sister happened to know Sayali and he promptly sent the address to MP. Sayali was completely floored by MP's involvement and now she was motivated to meet the man. All she had to do was persuade her dad to take her to Pune to meet her idol.

The place was found with some difficulty but soon she was with him, all excited and beaming to be with her hero. She told him that her dream in life was to become a doctor. MP told her, 'What one needs in life is single-minded determination, courage in the face of adversity, patience in the face of frustration and faith in the face of grief. So go for it girl, and God be with you!'

This meeting with her hero was, Sayali claims, the turning point in her life. 'It created the "hope for the best and be prepared for the worst" kind of attitude in me', she writes. 'It helped me realise my dream to become a doctor with an optimistic approach that is so helpful to the noble profession I pursue today.'

There were others who never met or spoke to MP, but were deeply inspired by him nevertheless.

> PARVATHY DEV Shyla was a young schoolgirl who read about MP in a weekend magazine while spending her summer holidays in Kerala at her grandfather's place. Intrigued and impressed, she asked her grandfather if he knew anything further about MP. 'Oh yes, his father is Panchapakesan, who was the president of our panchayat a few years ago', he replied. The little girl was too small to go looking for MP's home and soon returned to her parent's home.
>
> She couldn't get MP out of her mind, however, and decided to write him a letter, giving him her email address and contact details. Not knowing his address, she addressed the envelope to:
>
> MP Anil Kumar,
> S/O Mr Panchapakesan,
> Former Fighter Pilot, IAF,
> Khadki, Pune
>
> She had almost given up hope of a reply when one day an envelope arrived. Hands shaking, she opened the envelope and read the first

lines: 'Dear Parvathy, I received your letter the day before. What impressed me first is your calligraphy!' This was the beginning of a friendship that continued till his death.

The mails flew between them and as they grew closer, MP started calling her 'chatterbox'. She once asked him, 'Why did you choose to be a fighter pilot? Isn't it too risky?' MP replied, 'How many accidents occur on our highways everyday and how many of them are fatal? People do not stay at home fearing accidents, do they?' Based on MP's motivation and guidance, she went on to do her majors in music and finally took up a job as an announcer on radio. On hearing of the development, MP wrote back to her, 'It seems that people have stopped listening to any other radio other than the FM channel where Parvathy reads her news!'

Despite numerous opportunities that she had in her life to go and meet MP, Shyla could never pick up courage to go and meet MP face to face at the paraplegic home, a decision that she regrets till this day.

ADITI DHAR read about MP in a magazine at a dentist's waiting room, and wrote to him. Her husband was posted at the Air Force Academy. In the course of their correspondence she would send MP pressed flowers of the gulmohar, flame of the forest and silk cotton trees as they bloomed at the academy, to give him a feel of the place he had loved. Then they lost touch. Two years later, in 2000, when her son was swept away in an avalanche at 15,000 feet in the mountainous border areas, and she waited grief-stricken in a cold Delhi winter, she got a call from a stranger, saying that MP had asked him to trace her. 'I fell from the skies. Able persons who wanted to contact us hadn't been able to do so and here is a man in a wheelchair who makes contact!' she writes.

When she returned to Calcutta, a letter from Anil awaited her, a letter that tried to dull her pain. 'His mind was like a garden of innumerable flowers, each blooming with just the touch of his inspiration. A mind so effervescent, full of ideas and inspiration and a beautiful sense of humour', she concludes.

Over time, Aditi became busy with being a grandmother, stopped writing letters to Anil but continued to communicate with him over the internet, thanks to her daughter who helped her to get her messages across. She writes that one of her old uncles had a spinal problem and was unable to walk. Aditi was quick to tell him the MP story and gave him copies of his articles to read which gave the much-needed boost to the old man's morale and hope.

One day, her granddaughter came to her to ask for help to write a 'story with a difference' for a school project. Without batting an eyelid, she opened her mail and gave her Anil's story to write about!

'Hold the phone to his ears', said Nehal, sobbing uncontrollably. She wanted to hear him one last time. The attendant she spoke to had told her that he wasn't sure if MP would survive the next few hours. She had, therefore, requested her close friends from college days, Nikhar and Rohan, to go to the hospital and give her a firsthand report on MP's condition. They promptly sent her a couple of photographs, showing MP lying propped up, his mouth covered with an oxygen mask.

She now heard his laboured breathing and a grunt from MP suggested that she could be heard. 'Oh my Dodoe! I have never been so restless!' she began, 'It's so hard to see you in this condition, my Dodoe. I am sorry I can't be by your side now... I want to be next to you and hug you tight. I know you are waiting to fly away from me. In a way, I am happy... you soon will be free, at peace.' She sank to the floor as she said that and before disconnecting the line, mumbled between sobs, 'I love you Dodoe. I will miss you... and I shall be with you soon'. By morning, she got the message that MP was gone.

NEHAL KHOSLA was in the 9th grade, barely 15 in 2005, when her English teacher, Ms Primento, suggested the names of three persons whose stories were inspirational and a must-read—Sachin Tendulkar, Bachendri Pal and MP Anil Kumar. While the accomplishments of the first two were well known, an inquisitive

Nehal wanted to find out why MP Anil Kumar was being equated with these two greats and borrowed her senior's textbook to find out more. She could barely understand a little of the story, and walked up to her teacher asking her to explain in simpler English. Her eyes widened in fascination as the teacher narrated the story. She had found her new hero and wanted to meet him right away!

She put pen to paper and sought a meeting with him, but was unfortunate not to get his reply. It was almost a year after she was formally taught the chapter in class 10 that she wrote to MP again and got her first reply. Around that time, Nehal's little brother had won the 'best script writer' award for a children's film—'Love Changes Everything'—at the Toronto film festival. She now wanted to do a film on the hero of her life, with the help of her brother.

The proposal was sent to MP in a mail, which he promptly rejected. 'I am no hero. In fact, I am nowhere near as great as Mr Rajinder Johar of the 'Family of Disabled' who does so much for people like us and other famed paraplegics from the Army who have achieved wonders.... they are the ones about whom stories can be written and movies made.' Nehal refused to relent and a series of mails were exchanged. Finally, the entire Khosla family decided to visit Pune and convince MP.

'Most students leave my lair disenchanted for they find me a lousy guy vis-a-vis what's projected in the textbook. :-) :-) So, descend to good old terra firma... and prepare yourself to tryst with an uninteresting chap!', he wrote to Nehal prior to the visit. As soon as the family car stopped in the parking of the paraplegic home, Nehal jumped off and went looking for her hero, a bunch of flowers in her hand. MP sat at his desk pecking away at his keyboard when he saw the 16-year-old breeze into his room. A few awkward moments later, she went and hugged him. The chemistry was instant. Soon they both were best of friends and MP told her the story of his life from his school, NDA and his flying days in the IAF in the next few meetings. The besotted youngster also managed to chirp away the story of her life till then. 'While I was leaving the PRC, MP said, "Let me see whether you will remember me or the lines from Airborne to Chairborne after a few years"', writes Nehal. As the first meeting got over, the brother and sister were more than ever convinced to do the film. And over the next few meetings, Nehal continued to woo an obstinate MP about the film. She prepared a rough draft of the script and asked him for advice.

MP told her, 'I was secretly hoping that you had unceremoniously buried your documentary "misadventure"... but no, you intend to continue bullying this poor soul. I shall call you Bully from now on'. Prior to her visit one weekend, MP wrote to her, 'I may consider your proposal favourably if you promise to make me Kheer (not too sweet please) and Pizza and feed me when you come over tomorrow'. Feeding him while having big bites of the pizza herself the next day, Nehal recalls, MP told her, 'Since you are bullying me so much... Let's do it!'

Over the next couple of meetings, the shooting continued with a serving IAF officer playing the role of MP prior to the accident and MP playing himself for the rest of the story. In my talks with MP, he told me how all the takes and retakes left him pretty exhausted but he played along for the sake of the children.

Only editing was left when the entire project was shelved since the children could not get someone to sponsor the production costs which, even for a small film, were turning out to be prohibitive. The film, in parts, is lying somewhere with the cameraman and efforts are on to retrieve it.

After the edit of this book had been completed, I accidently met a young girl, Aarti, at Dehradun through a common friend. As we spoke, I happened to tell her that I was writing a biography on a quadriplegic. 'MP Anil Kumar??!!' was her immediate reaction, surprising me. Then she poured out the story of how she was alive and happy all due to the chapter that she read in her textbook long ago.

'I READ the chapter 'airborne to chairborne' in my text book a day before it was to be covered in class and did not understand a word of the high flown language. That was why our teacher had asked us to get our dictionaries to school I realised', said Aarti. The teacher went on to explain the chapter over two days after which all in the class were completely mesmerised, she remembers. The lesson was never forgotten and she continued to read it over and over again over the next few years after she went through a personal tragedy of losing her father, who was the only bread winner of the family.

'I derived strength from the chapter which I had carefully torn from my textbook as I went on with the tough times of growing up without a father', she said to me.

Time flew and the chapter was all but forgotten as she settled down in life and in a job. She now made plans to settle down with the man she fell in love with at work. As the days to get married neared, she realised that she was being cheated. Devastated, she walked out of the job and the city that she lived in, to find solace at her ancestral home in the outskirts of Mumbai. She went into bouts of depression and even contemplated ending her life. To take her mind off the matter, she picked up an old book to read amongst the many at her ancestral home. A rumpled sheaf of papers tucked away inside the book fell out into her lap. It was the chapter torn out from her text book.

'As I read through the chapter again, I realised that I needed to look forward and get along with life. It was not as bad as my mentor MP had gone through. I steeled myself and I felt a change in my attitude towards the incident. I soon moved out to Dehradun for a new job where I found my new life waiting for me', she told to me.

SUBBALAKSHMI SURAMPUDI was married to an old school boy from Sainik School Kazhakootam. Cleaning some old piles of books belonging to her husband one day, she came across the OBA Magazine and took time off to leaf through it. As she flipped through it, the mouth written article 'Airborne to Chairborne' stared at her in the face. She read and re-read the article, sitting transfixed in between heaps of books. The article was ingrained in her mind and she was determined to meet MP at the first opportunity. On an official visit to Pune in 1996, she made her way to Anil's room not really having a clue about what or whom she was going to meet. 'As I ventured into the computer room, Anil, with a quizzical look in his eyes, motioned to me, with his pencil going up and down in his mouth, to come in.' She started, 'I read about you in a magazine that I found in my house which belongs to one Babu Narayan…' She had not even finished the sentence when the pencil dropped into his lap and the connect established. They went on to give each other details of each other's life as the evening turned to night. 'This became a habit with me on every visit of mine to Pune. I even introduced some more of my friends to MP too', she writes. 'After each meeting I would go out wiser on topics as varied as politics, fighter aircrafts and international relations. He also spoke of his accident and disability, but there were no signs of regret or remorse', she remembers.

She once took her husband, a Malayalee from Trivandrum, to meet MP. As soon as MP saw the man, he burst out, 'Oh so you are the one! I remember you from the rival football team and we have played a match against each other while we were in school!!'

Later, when the couple decided to adopt a baby girl, they went to MP for advice. His immediate response was, 'I am a strong proponent of adoption, since it changes life of at least three people'. He was very pleased to see the girl and often mailed the couple to find out how she was being 'brought up' by the new parents! Later on, Lakshmi made sure that their daughter got to meet MP while she grew up. MP would always wait for her with chocolates and often advise her on what books to read. The seven year old would reciprocate her love by singing for him a few Malayalam songs.

She concludes her mail to me, 'In any overwhelming hardship, he comes to my mind, inevitably. Can any crisis be bigger than his? I take inspiration from the knowledge that such a person did really exist. I am happy about the favourable coincidences that made our friendship possible. He stands as the assurance that there is the potential of a phoenix in every human being. I met him by chance and this chance has made so much of difference in my life'.

AND THERE were those, like Ashla Krishnan, who he touched even after he was gone. Ashla is a quadriplegic. Daughter of a retired sergeant of the IAF, she and her mother settled in Kannur, after his demise. She is an MCA graduate and worked as an IT professional prior to her accident. She writes, 'I was working in Chennai at the time and I fell off a running train while travelling back to Chennai after a vacation'. She was taken by some villagers to a hospital where she lay unconscious for three days before being taken to a specialist hospital for surgery. Her company was kind enough to allow her to

> work from home after the accident which left her paralysed.
>
> One morning her regular newspaper was not delivered, and she asked her mother to get her a different newspaper to read. 'I read about the demise of a certain MP Anil Kumar on the front page, a person I hadn't even heard about', she writes. Intrigued, she scoured the internet for all the information she could gather on him and, in no time, she had read almost everything he had written. 'It filled me with a confidence that I cannot describe in words and I decided to join the "MP Anil Kumar: An Inspiration" Facebook page.' She also put up a post saying that she wanted help with rehabilitation.
>
> Some of Anil's friends searched for a rehabilitation centre as well as an occupation for her and managed to get in touch with Rajagopal, a retired professor of a medical college, who headed a palliative care centre in Trivandrum. Ashla was told to contact Dr Rajagopal. He employed her as his personal assistant and a full-time volunteer at Pallium India.

Today Ashla leads a meaningful life and lives with her mother on the premises of the institution, devoting all her energies to her work. 'It was God's blessings and Anil Sir's soul that helped me,' she wrote in her mail to me. When I suggested to her to help me set up an "MP Anil Kumar Foundation" to look after the paraplegics of India, she was excited and more than willing to help. MP described Ganga Devi as one of his closest friends. Although they had never met, they were online friends for seven years. 'I never got to meet Anil and that's my bad luck', she said to me, quickly adding, 'But I am lucky enough to have interacted with him and known him well enough'.

SHE FIRST read about MP in the Malayalam daily *Matrubhumi* in 2007. The next day she did a Google search and found out all she could about him and sat down to write to him. She traced MP's email id through the editor of *Matrubhumi* and the writer of the article. She wrote to him on May 22, and received a reply on the 25th.

Ganga had suffered a personal tragedy and she found in Anil an empathetic shoulder to cry on. Anil wrote back to her, 'Having lost everything in life barring my brain, I have only this to say: Look forward in life and don't live in the past as clutching on to past memories will turn life melancholic'.

As time flew like the mails between them, Ganga also started advising him on topics to write on. She urged him to write about his hospital experiences and to publish an anthology of all his articles for the world to read. She also became a critique on all the topics that he wrote about and eagerly waited for his articles to appear in some media or the other. MP too would wait for her comments and the series of mails would thus start between the two discussing the subject threadbare.

During one such discussion on the topic of euthanasia, MP wrote to her, 'Mercy killing doesn't mean every cripple has to be euthanised or every plug of life support system needs to be pulled—it is meant for those who do not wish to prolong the suffering'. Later, in another of his mails, he writes, 'I do not want to scare you with the horror stories and compulsions of quadriplegics. I do not expect the nation to think about people like us since we are an agglomeration of conservative societies'. One of his mails to Ganga reads thus, 'I've suffered enough. My greatest wish today is for a peaceful and painless death, on my own bed, not on a hospital bed—hopefully without ever having to get admitted in a hospital'. Then he adds, '*Unfortunately, life can only be understood backwards, but it must be lived forwards. Life is nothing but an adventure with its share of hurdles, sorrows and hopes, with partial successes here and there*'.

In 2011, Ganga realised that MP was not keeping too well. He kept falling sick with minor ailments and was losing weight, she noticed from the photographs she received from Anil and his friends. She received the last mail from him in March 2014. After that there was silence.

I wish I could pen down more of the anecdotes like these that were sent to me. But my literary advisors tell me that they are more or less the same and you the reader may get bored with the overdose. So I guess we should get into the epilogue now.

End note

I FIRST saw signs of MP slowing down as early as 2011. He told me that he was catching infections too often, followed by low-grade fever which left him rather exhausted. His reading and writing on the net also decreased. He said to me one day, 'Somehow I cannot read for too long, neither can I sit in front of the computer...I feel tired too soon. I would rather take care now than get admitted to the hospital. I simply hate the thought of being there'.

He said that he was reminded of how one of his friends had taken MP's medical documents to a specialist abroad for a second opinion a few years ago. Having seen the papers and read them in detail, the doctor wanted to know when the patient had died. 'Oh no!' exclaimed the friend who had taken the papers. 'This man is very much alive and doing so much meaningful work.'

Now it was the specialist's turn to be surprised. He couldn't believe that a man with this extent of disability had survived so long.

While he was in the ICU, MP had been telling BS Krishna Kumar not to make too much of a splash about his illness. He didn't want people landing up at the hospital to express their concern. But when he was gone, the news spread like wildfire over the internet. Phones rang all over the network of friends across the country. The news of the passing of the legend was flashed in all the major dailies and local television channels in Pune and Kerala.

The funeral was planned at the Bopodi crematorium the next day. Krishna Kumar writes, 'The body was taken out of the mortuary in the morning; I had one last look—he lay motionless as he did for most of his life. The only thing missing on his face was his characteristic smile'. The body, now draped in the air force flag, was taken to the PRC which had been his home for the last quarter-century. The inmates on their wheelchairs gathered around the casket and paid their last respects. He had been the greatest motivation in their life and they were tearful to see him go.

As the body reached the crematorium, there was a large crowd waiting already there to say its last goodbye. There was a healthy representation from the Army, Navy and the Air Force, besides a large number of school children and civilian friends of Anil. Some retired senior officers of the Armed Forces were also present. Wreaths were laid on behalf of the Chief of Air Staff, the General Officer Commanding, South Western Army Command,

and the Air Officer Commanding of the South Western Air Command based at Gandhinagar. Breaking tradition, friends spoke about MP to the gathering as is done at Christian funerals, paying tribute to the departed soldier. Some in the crowd were weeping uncontrollably. MP had touched so many lives.

A contingent of Air Warriors in full regalia gave a ceremonial salute of reverse arms. The draped IAF flag was smartly removed from the body, folded in a military manner, and handed over to MP's brother. The military part of the ceremony over, the body was bedecked in flowers and the traditional cremation rites were taken over by the priests from the Pune Sreenarayaneeyar Society.

Amidst the chanting of mantras, the body slowly moved into the electric furnace. Krishna writes, 'I almost heard MP saying with a glow in his eyes, "Come on guys, it's only my body that's gone, my spirit will live on forever. Don't weep and grieve over me... Move on... and touch the sky with glory". The furnace reminded me of the reheat (afterburners) on Anil's MiG. He was now rolling down the runway for takeoff. He moved into eternity, leaving indelible imprints on many hearts and minds'.

'Ike' Isenhower writes in his obituary, 'Anil came into this world with a purpose, accomplished it better than the best and joined the stars. After all, he was a darling son, a loving brother, a brilliant student, a talented sportsman, an erudite academician, an extraordinary combatant, a diehard crusader... and best of all... a humane human being. A man on a short term lease to us lesser mortals'.

One of my friends to whom I gave the script for an independent opinion wrote to me, 'I don't want to sound clichéd but MP inspired people—*Jindagi ke saath bhi-Jindagi ke baad bhi!.* He has motivated me to spend some of my time and energy in making a difference to peoples' lives... like the squirrels in the Ramayana who carried small stones for a big cause... I wish I had seen him alive'.

I am so grateful to have known him.

MP Anil Kumar just after commissioning

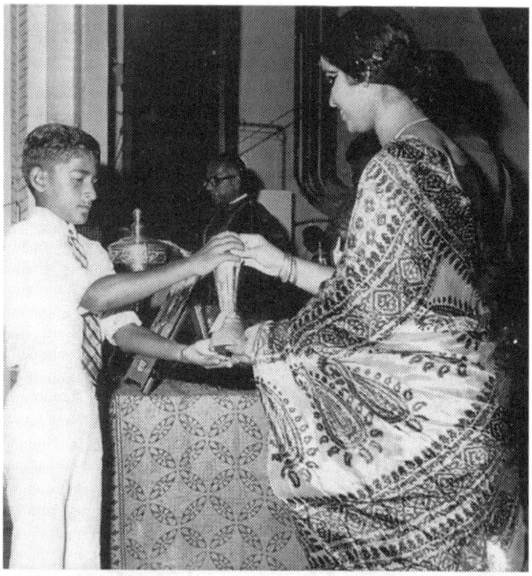

Receiving awards in middle school

In 6th Class, with Principal and Staff of the school

Receiving a prize at high school

In class 12, in front of his Instructor's residence

With fellow cadets of the NCC during a camp

NDA, 6th term at camp

In VIth term, with the first flying instructors at the NDA

At the Passing Out parade at NDA, Khadakwasla, Dec 1983. Saluting the Quarter Deck

Final Dining-in-Night, December 1983. Book Prize award winners

In the Iskra trainer cockpit at Hakimpet during advanced flying training

Atop an MiG-21, Pathankot

With fellow pilots in Pathankot, MP's first posting

Receiving a performance award (L); On advanced training visit to Leh

At a squadron get-together

Receiving 'fully ops' certificate at 3 Sqn at Pathankot

Receiving the 'Best in aerobatics' trophy at the Commissioning Parade-AFA, 21 Dec 1984

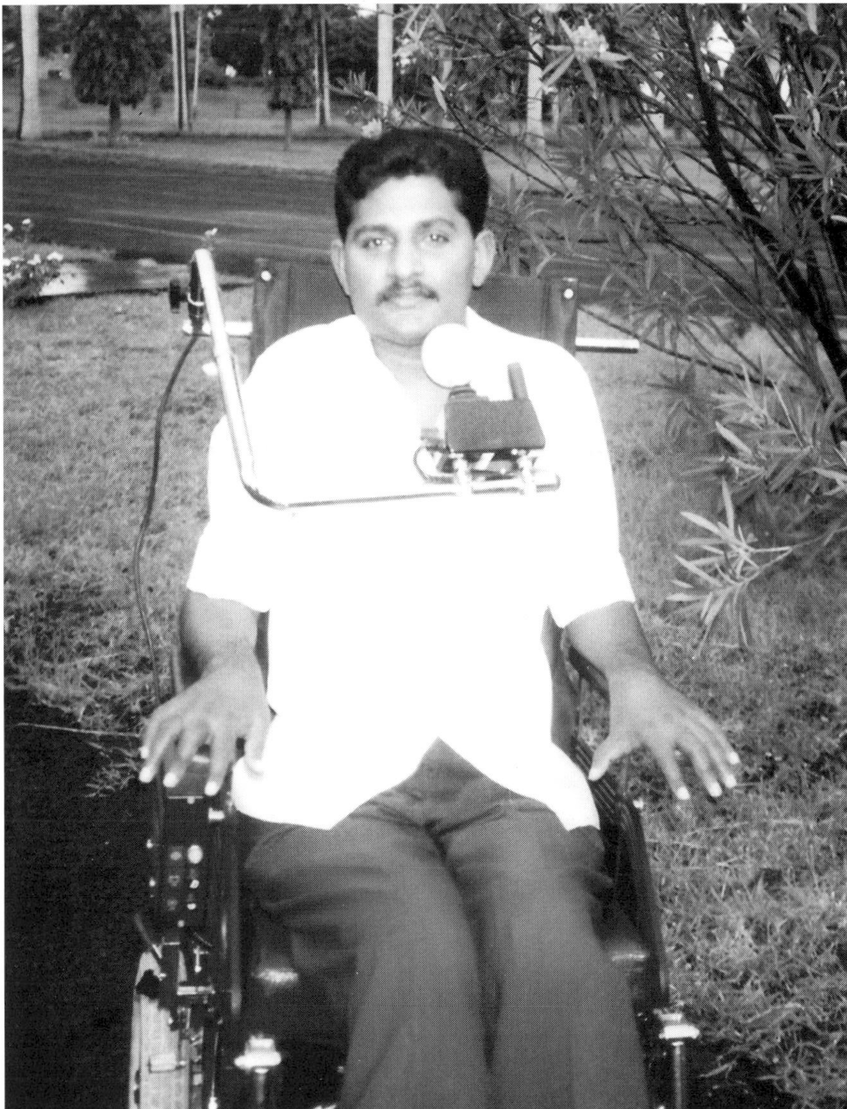

In his chin-operated wheel chair at the PRC

At the Airforce station, Pune

Down but not out, at the rehabilitation centre

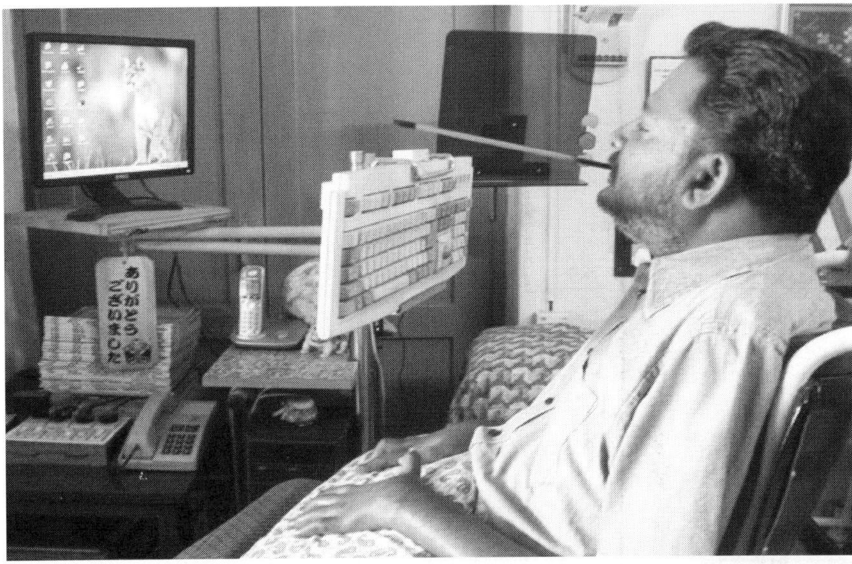

Stephen Hawking moments

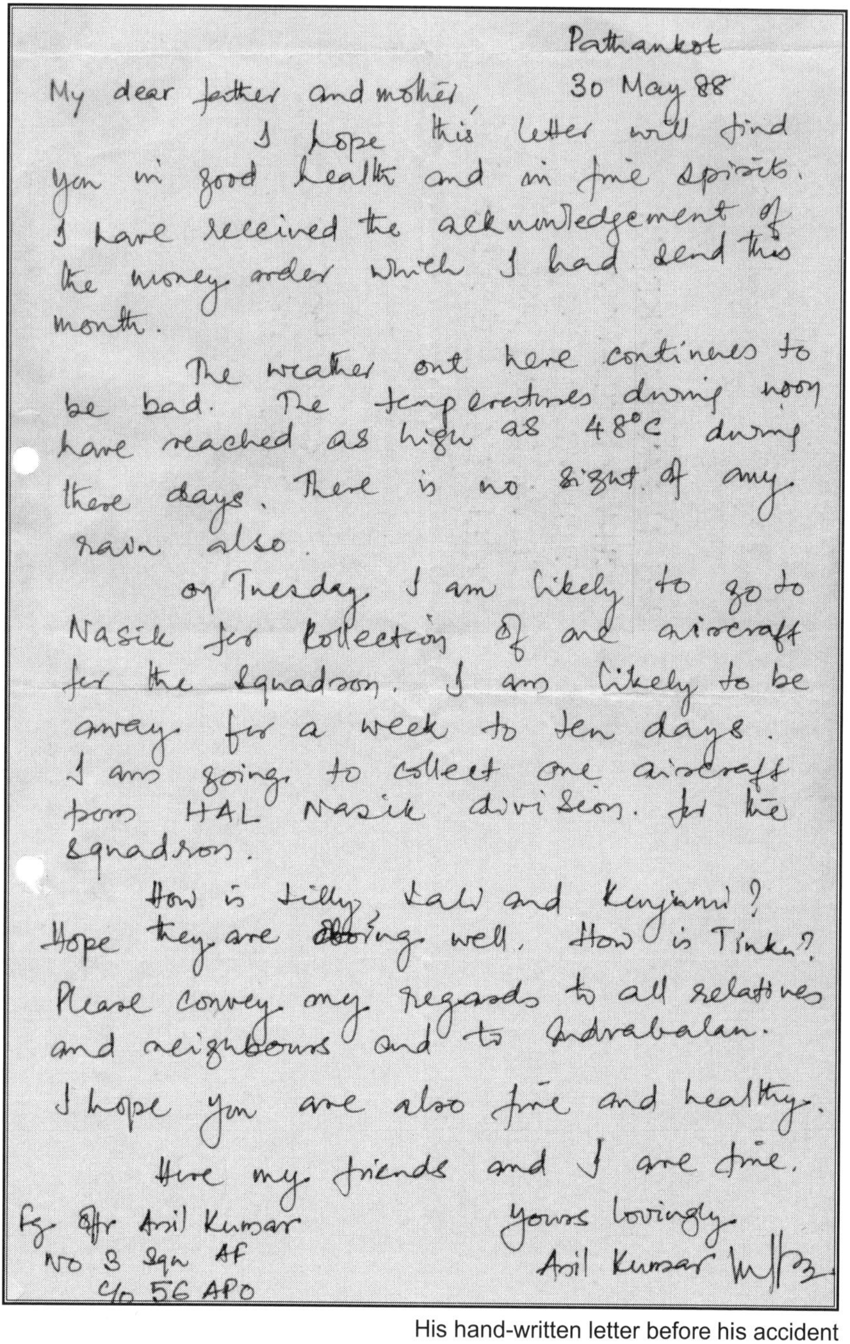

Pathankot
30 May 88

My dear father and mother,

I hope this letter will find you in good health and in fine spirits. I have received the acknowledgement of the money order which I had send this month.

The weather out here continues to be bad. The temperatures during noon have reached as high as 48°C during these days. There is no sight of any rain also.

On Tuesday I am likely to go to Nasik for collection of one aircraft for the squadron. I am likely to be away for a week to ten days. I am going to collect one aircraft from HAL Nasik division. for the squadron.

How is Jilly, Lali and Kunjunni? Hope they are doing well. How is Tinku? Please convey my regards to all relatives and neighbours and to Indrabalan.

I hope you are also fine and healthy.

Here my friends and I are fine.

Yours lovingly
Anil Kumar

Fg Offr Anil Kumar
No 3 Sqn AF
C/o 56 APO

His hand-written letter before his accident

Kirkee 15/x/92

Dear father,

I received your letter two days ago. Brother Ravi came here on 5th and handed over the items. I'm glad to hear about the change of attitude in Usari. So, the marriage season is on.

I read in the newspaper about the deluge inundating South Kerala and the unfortunate loss of life and property. I hope all is well over there. On 10th & 11th we too experienced heavy rains.

Yesterday Sathyaseelan annan came here. He may take leave in December to complete the house construction.

My days roll on in the old way.

Any news from Ajith Kr (Koonthallor)? Sincerely. Anil

M. D. Anilkumar

Tel : 57271/585

Paraplegic Home,
Park Road, Kirkee,
Pune-411 020.

24 Jan

Dear father,

I received your letter on 21st. I am enclosing the DD worth Rs 50,000/-. This amount is part of my PF. Please devote this entire sum towards Lilly's marriage in which ever fashion you deem fit viz purchase of garments, ornaments etc or otherwise. Bro. Ravi came here on the 12th evening and handed over the items. Bro. Omi is at present in TVM to be available there for his daughters operation. You should be aware of one Dr Muralidharan Nair, from Nulamood. His younger brother is in the CAF as a med. offr. He had written to me. With regards to pensions, I've just despatched my pension papers. It should take some more time. This year we had a severe winter. I'm okay. I hope the same, there. Nothing more.

yours faithfully,

anil

His mouth-written letters

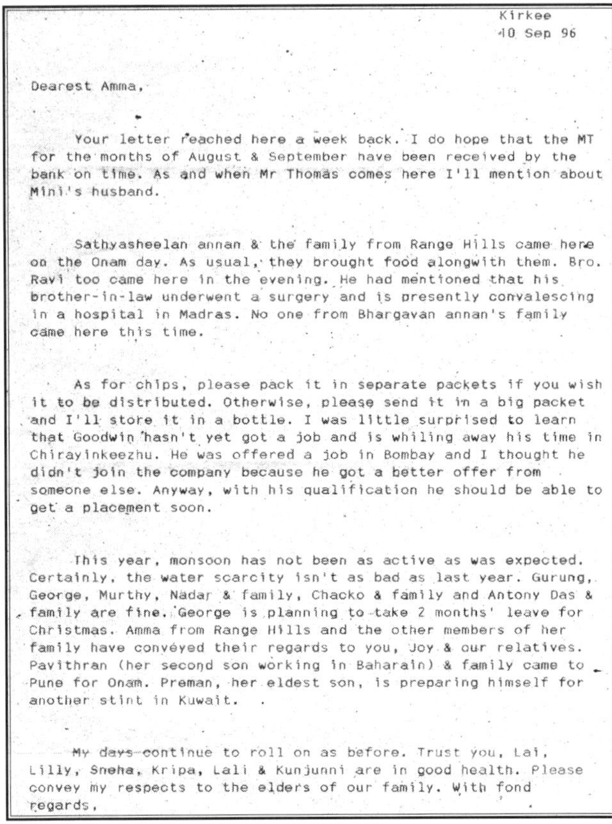

Kirkee
10 Sep 96

Dearest Amma,

Your letter reached here a week back. I do hope that the MT for the months of August & September have been received by the bank on time. As and when Mr Thomas comes here I'll mention about Mini's husband.

Sathyasheelan annan & the family from Range Hills came here on the Onam day. As usual, they brought food alongwith them. Bro. Ravi too came here in the evening. He had mentioned that his brother-in-law underwent a surgery and is presently convalescing in a hospital in Madras. No one from Bhargavan annan's family came here this time.

As for chips, please pack it in separate packets if you wish it to be distributed. Otherwise, please send it in a big packet and I'll store it in a bottle. I was little surprised to learn that Goodwin hasn't yet got a job and is whiling away his time in Chirayinkeezhu. He was offered a job in Bombay and I thought he didn't join the company because he got a better offer from someone else. Anyway, with his qualification he should be able to get a placement soon.

This year, monsoon has not been as active as was expected. Certainly, the water scarcity isn't as bad as last year. Gurung, George, Murthy, Nadar & family, Chacko & family and Antony Das & family are fine. George is planning to take 2 months' leave for Christmas. Amma from Range Hills and the other members of her family have conveyed their regards to you, Joy & our relatives. Pavithran (her second son working in Baharain) & family came to Pune for Onam. Preman, her eldest son, is preparing himself for another stint in Kuwait.

My days continue to roll on as before. Trust you, Lai, Lilly, Sneha, Kripa, Lali & Kunjunni are in good health. Please convey my respects to the elders of our family. With fond regards,

This is a typed letter when he got a computer

Author with Anil's mother and sisters

The Sainik School building; the motivating Harward aircraft at school

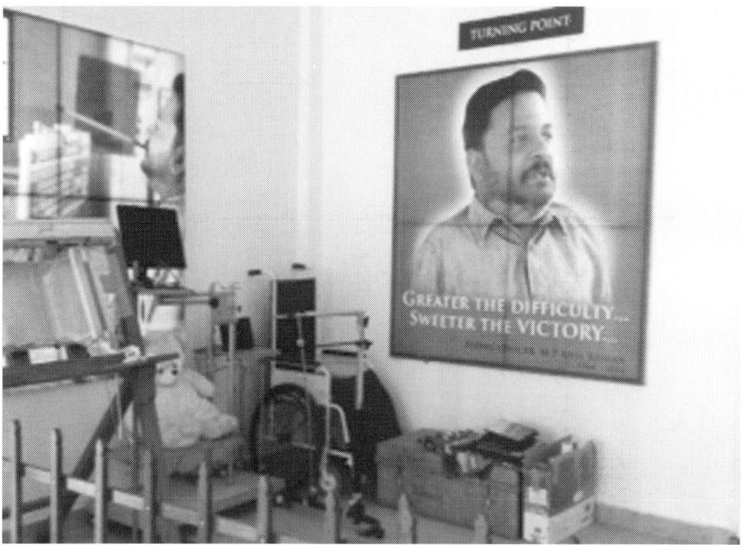

The dedicated school space in rememberence

Anil's room in Chirayinkeezhu

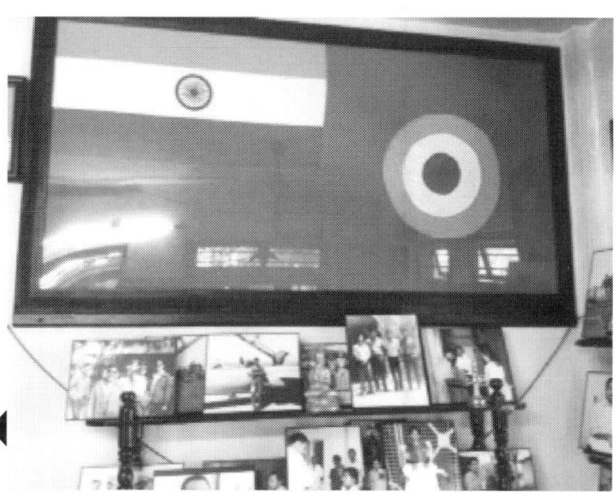

The Airforce flag that draped Anil's body is displayed in his room

CONTEST III TURNING POINT IN MY LIFE

Third Anniversary Special

Turning Point

When entries for the *Turning Point* kept pouring on our desk, they stirred our hearts. Poignant tales that changed the course of our readers' lives gave an insight into how – when the going gets tough, the tough get going. The shattered fabric of life, due to the sudden death of a near and dear one, is steadily woven with the precious threads of steel and grit, of patience and perseverance. The jolt that was a bit too much to bear, becomes the very foundation on which a new castle is built, one on which the individual or family stands in unison.

Besides personal tragedies that are sure to move your heart, readers have written about change in their attitudes, after a particular incident that happened in their lives. We reproduce ten entries, including the three prize-winning ones.

The most touching entry we received was from young Anil Kumar, who was a brilliant cadet at the National Defence Academy but has been confined to a wheelchair after a tragic accident, soon after he was commissioned as an officer. Imagine this young boy's state of mind when he was paralysed neck, downwards. Today, he is residing at the Paraplegic Home in Khadki and is unable to use his limbs. But he has not given up. With a dogged determination he has learnt to use his mouth for writing.

He has sent us his prize-winning entry by penning down his soul-stirring story – with his mouth. We couldn't believe it could be so beautifully written, when we received his entry – as you will see, it is so neatly written. We confirmed this with the Paraplegic Home and were stunned to know that Anil had actually written it himself. Hats off to this brave young man for the courage of his convictions. We are sure that each one of you who reads his story will derive inspiration from him. We produce his letter, *ad verbatim*.

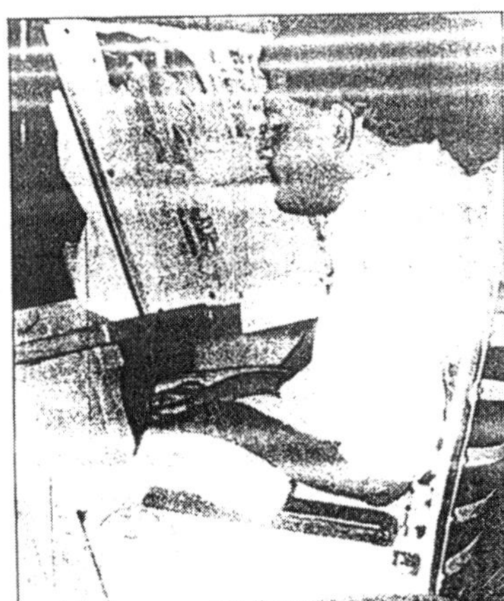

Anil Kumar.

30

Indian Express - CITIZEN

This is what *The Indian Express* newspaper wrote, publishing MP Anil Kumar's entry for a contest, on October 11, 1994

Third Anniversary Special

CONTEST III TURNING POINT IN MY LIFE

FIRST PRIZE
Rs.500/-

AIRBORNE TO CHAIRBORNE

My attempts to move my limbs ended futilely. The pain in the neck was excruciating and intensifying by the second. I was stumped for a moment but quickly recovered to realise the seriousness and significance of my inability to get up.

I do not remember whether I involuntarily screamed, then, in sheer desperation. My mental state on that abominable night of 28 June 88 was a medley of intense frustration, utmost dejection and extreme disappointment. At around 2300 hrs, whilst returning to the Officers Mess after night flying, I drove onto a wooden road barrier - just ahead of the technical area gate inside Air Force Station, Pathankot. The impact wrenched my neck and broke the cervical spine. The injury resulted in total paralysis below the neck with no limb movements whatsoever. After overnight's stay in Military Hospital (MH) Pathankot I was transferred to Army Hospital, Delhi (AHDC). Neck surgery failed to mitigate my predicament. Though I had brief spells of consciousness I do not recollect various incidents and my fight for survival during the fortnight's hospitalisation

contd...

MP Anil Kumar's entry for the contest in *The Indian Express* which bagged the first prize

Third Anniversary Special

at AHRC. On 12 July 88, I was transferred to the Spinal Cord Injury Centre (SCIC) of MH Kirkee. Two weeks after my admission, I gathered my wits and eagerly inquired about the prognosis. The medical officer looked up into the false ceiling and motioned his hands skywards; perhaps, he wanted me to adjure divine intervention. This charade instantly deflated my hopes but it conveyed the enormity and hopelessness of the incurable nature of the incapacitation. Inconsistencies of life have always bemused me but not even the wildest nightmare presaged that one day I would fall prey to such a quirk of fate. The modicum of faith I had in Providence got shattered when I failed to show even an iota of improvement.

The cervical spinal injury (quadriplegia) necessitated me to lead a totally dependent life tethered to the bed and wheelchair. It wasn't just loss of tactile inputs and outputs but absolute dependency on someone else to accomplish mundane necessities and domestic chores; even swabbing ears and swatting flies. Dystrophy set in within couple of months and took its toll by altering the geometry of torso and limbs. The mirror replicated the image.

contd...

CONTEST III TURNING POINT

of a human skeleton swathed by a layer of wizened skin. Depression to some extent and numerous encumbrances forced me to while away two years in MH Kirkee. Nonetheless, I learned to dissemble and with a smile on the face I managed to hide the pangs of the heart. The Indian Air Force (IAF) realised my uselessness and discharged me from service on 12 Apr 90. That silly accident dealt the coup de grace to my aspirations and career in the IAF. In Aug 90, at the young age of 26, I got admitted to Paraplegic Home, Kirkee, Pune as an inmate to begin the second phase of my life – afresh.

I was born and brought up in a hamlet by name Chirayinkil, 85 kms north of Trivandrum. At the age of 9, I entered Sainik School, Kazhakootam. A slow learner and an unobtrusive performer by nature, I ~~gradually got my engine of performance well oiled and well maintained to~~ consistently excelled in both academics and sports. Later, I was found worthy enough to be adjudged as the best Air Force cadet of 65th course at NDA, Khadakwasla and as the best in Aerobatics at the passing out parade of 134 pilots course at Air Force

contd...

CONTEST III TURNING POINT

Third Anniversary Special

Academy Secunderabad. In Dec 84, I was commissioned into the IAF as a fighter pilot.

All my attempts to rationalise personal catastrophes have always mystified and at times stupefied me. Anyway, I had to break the self-imposed stupor to adapt to the new challenges posed by the debility. Therefore, in Sep 90 I decided to learn the art of writing by holding a pen in my mouth (because of dysfunctional hands). I began by illegibly scribbling alphabets but was chagrined to find little progress even after 3 weeks' laborious efforts. One day I decided to change tactics and write a proper letter to Sheela George, the person who kept on chivvying to start mouth-writing (earlier, I had paid very little attention to her exhortation). My joy knew no bounds when I decipherably completed few lines which embodied my first mouth-written letter. Initially, I found my hard work to be a pie in the sky but 4 to 5 months' assiduous efforts resulted in achieving a readable style of writing. This modest achievement helped me a great deal by reviving the chain of correspondence and begetting new friends!

In May 91, I was presented as

contd...

electrically operated wheelchair with chin controls for manoeuvring (imported from U.K.), thanks to the benevolence of the IAF. Motorised mobility, though only a substitute for natural one, has enlivened my lifestyle.

It was Wg. Cdr. Murlidharan, my former flight commander, who first mooted the use of a computer as a writing tool to assist me to exploit my mental faculty to the hilt. Wg. Cdr R.V. Jog (retd.) and Dr. A. Kulkarni besides teaching programming did the spadework of exploring the possibilities of a PC acquisition, by entreating some PC manufacturers to modify the keyboard to cater for my mouth-operation — sadly, to no avail. Needless to say that their apathy emasculated my resolve and ultimately in Feb 92, we had no choice but to discontinue the scheme.

In the meantime, I toyed with the idea of teaching. For some untenable reasons I kept declining the offers (by bringing one imaginary reason or the other as an ad hoc excuse). Aforesaid setbacks notwithstanding, I am very hopeful of making the second phase of life as meaningful as the one I would have had

contd...

CONTEST III TURNING POINT IN MY LIFE

Third Anniversary Special

from the confine of a cockpit

Believe it or not, every dark cloud has a silver lining. To surmount even seemingly insuperable barriers one has to shun the thought of disability and muster the remnant faculties and canalise one's energies purposefully and whole-heartedly. It isn't just physical ability and intelligence but an insatiable appetite for success and an unstinted will power that would [illegible] the warp and woof of the fabric called human destiny. Greater the difficulty sweeter the victory.

M. P. ANIL KUMAR
PARAPLEGIC HOME
KIRKEE
PUNE 411 020

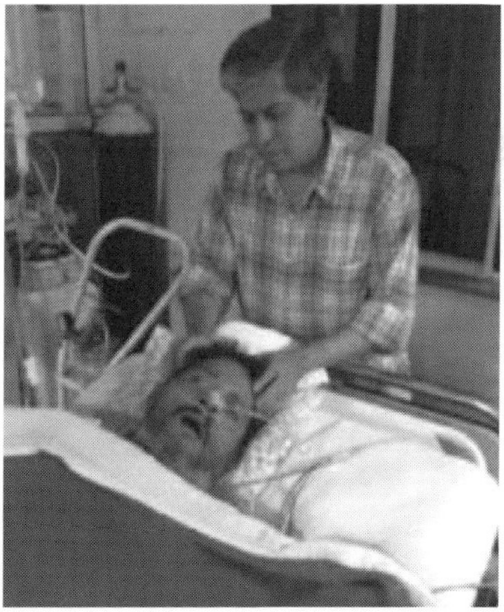

Shrikrishna, who was beside MP Anil Kumar just a few days before his end, writes in a letter to himself emailed at 21:00 hrs on 18 May from Lohegaon airport:

MP Anilkumar

What a man. Remembers every detail. When I conveyed the love and hugs from Nitin, Nandu, Nilu, Vishnu, Ram, Sharad.. he suddenly asked me to show him a photo of Sharad. Said, I haven't met him for so long. Thanks to FB I could show MP a photo of Sharad. He was thrilled.

I am torn.... MP asked me how long are you here.. .you are a free bird. That is MP telling me to stay longer. Subtle and soft. But the doctors cannot allow me to be with him all the time. I don't know how to tell him I have to go back to Bangalore.

His friend Col Kuriakose is speaking to MP now. He too is a wheelchair-bound soldier. Hepter accident in 1996 at ASTE Bangalore left him with permanent disabilities. Some classmates have requested that I should not post any photos of MP as they do not wish to remember him in this utter state. I value the sentiment. Hence I will not post photos.

I said I love you MP, and he says...I love you too. I have tears in my eyes....how to avoid this. Impossible. He also said he enjoys the head massages I give him very much. All visitor friends, do touch him, and if you can, massage his head.

Must head out to the airport now...never felt this utterly helpless....

O' Divine forces...please help MP. Please.